A Uniquely Powerful Approach To

Build an Online Business In 24 Hours

Enabling Entrepreneurs to Bring Their Businesses Online In No-Time

Shahram G. Maralani

Edition 1.1

Shahram G. Maralani
August 2020, The Netherlands
sm@shahrammaralani.com

Disclaimer
This publication is intended to help the readers in defining and acting on their digital transformation roadmaps building or transforming their online businesses and is only meant as educational substance. While the publisher has made every attempt to verify that the information provided in this book is correct and up to date, the publisher assumes no responsibility for any error, inaccuracy, or omission. The recommendations, examples, and solutions shared herein are not meant for every situation. The content is not intended to guarantee you achieve your envisioned results, and the publisher makes no such guarantee. The publisher shall not be liable for damages arising therefrom as business success is determined by many factors not limited to the content of this book. These may include market conditions, your potential to invest, your dedication, your actions, your available resources and more. Do not use this book as legal or financial advice. Instead use legal and financial professionals to evaluate your specific business situation.

Table of Contents

Introduction

Why I Wrote This Book

I work in a leadership role in a company called DNV GL. During my free time, I do research and write on how today's entrepreneurship world works. I investigate how successful startups come to exist and study how the great ones remain in Business over many years, some becoming multi-million businesses only over a few years. I also look into how the corporate world can benefit from similar principles and practices through Intrapreneurship. I do analyze the competences, specially the digital ones needed today to succeed as an Entrepreneur or Intrapreneur.

The business world as we know it today, has been through substantial changes over the last two decades. Looking at most of the companies sitting these days at the top of the charts, you realize that either they did not exist two decade ago or have been growing significantly only since then to arrive at where they are today. The names like Airbnb, Apple, Amazon, Uber, Spotify and Booking.com are just few examples of either of the two groups. On the other hand, there are some of the smaller businesses such as local shops and other local businesses who are extremely more successful than some of other competitors of them. You always find that supermarket or the butcher which is extremely successful or one single do-it-yourself shop which is going significantly beyond what other players are able to achieve.

Most of the principles and practices that such large or small companies have been putting in place, can be applied to any company in any industry. But what are those necessary ingredients for a business to arrive at where these companies are? Is it about the sector, or the niche they have been focusing on? Is it the design of their business model which embeds a magic formula of success into their operations? Did they build their business differently compared to the others? What is the magic that made these companies grow much more than their competitors who even sometimes may have products with the same or better quality or functionality? What systems do these companies put in place to cater for the need of a business of this size? What type of automations makes it possible to serve billions of people on the planet with such a seamless experience?

These are the question to which, I seek answers. And the answers are many. But there is one answer which explains the success for many of the companies I do study. This one answer has been the single reason for the existence of some of the world's newest corporations, an enabler for rejuvenation of some of the older multinationals, and a significant differentiator for many other smaller businesses. That one single answer explains the reason why I have written this book.

In addition, the global crisis of 2020 caused by the corona pandemic has created a new reality for people, businesses, societies, and countries. Although digitalization through building or transforming to an **online business** has been the buzz word since years in the different forums, the real actions for some of the organizations did not start before the pressure caused by this crisis. In the none-IT sectors of the corporate world, the limited knowledge and lack of real motivation – or market driver - together with the lack of agility in utilizing eventual insights and implementing eventual learnings have been preventing the creation of genuine business value through digitalization efforts, hence delaying transformation. For solo-entrepreneurs and Small to medium enterprises (SME's) on the other hand, imagining Digital Transformation and Building An Online Business as a monster and lack of knowledge on how simple but robust tools can help to go online in no time, have prevented earlier moves. The consequences show themselves in two folds. From one hand, there are businesses of any size going bankrupt one after another. On the other hand, other companies grow even during the crisis times such as the one in 2020, some even reaching to their all-time-high results. Looking at these companies there are two main factors making all the difference: first, which industry they are in. second, how online their business models are.

I have written this book to address this second factor which is also the answer to the questions above. The key audience of this book are Entrepreneurs like you who want to bring their businesses online or improve their already online businesses 'performance, or 'To-Be Entrepreneurs 'who do want to establish their first business, online from the beginning, as well as Intrapreneurs who look for a simple but robust manner to start online journey of their organizations. In this book, I focus mostly on solutions and recommendations fit for smaller businesses and solo-entrepreneurs, although most of the recommendations in this book are also applicable to businesses with a larger size. There are shops, restaurants, small companies, and more that are suffering from the crisis of 2020. I dedicate this book mainly to them to give some motivation in bringing their businesses online in no-time. At the same time, the process and the recommendations of this book are not meant only for this period of time and can be applied by entrepreneurs and intrapreneurs at any point in time in the future as the trend started since a decade and significantly intensified in 2020, will be there for a foreseeable future.

I hope you find this book an inspiration in creating success in your organizations, businesses, and societies by employing what the affordable and reachable technologies of today have to offer.

Enjoy reading!

Shahram G. Maralani
August 2020, The Netherlands

Build An Online Business in 24 Hours Free Companion Course

This is a **dynamic book**. By purchasing this book, you have also gotten access to all its future updates which I may create once in a while. I will add content, review, and update the existing ones and provide more strategies and techniques over time. All this will be at your reach, at no additional cost!

This book comes with a FREE companion course. During reading the book, you will see references to the content sitting in the companion course. To access the course contents, the companion workbook, the business ideation worksheet and to be able to benefit from all future updates and enhancements of this book, remember to register your book by signing up for the companion course.

URL:

https://shahrammaralani.teachable.com/p/build-an-online-business-in-24-hours/

You can also access the course from my website:

www.shahrammaralani.com

You can complete the book also without the companion course. But you will find additional information and some multimedia content which is intended to enhance your learning experience.

Chapter 1 - The Why

Why You Should Read This Book

Hello, and welcome in joining me on this journey to Build an Online Business in 24 hours. You may ask yourself: 'why am I here? Why did I pick this book to read? 'Let me try to help you to find a right answer. You are perhaps an Entrepreneur having experience in building, growing, and advancing one or multiple businesses for years. Or you are probably new to the world of entrepreneurship and in the process of starting your first venture. Or maybe you are a senior professional working as an Intrapreneur in the corporate world looking into the next best strategic move for your organization and yourself.

Have you recently been hearing that some of the Businesses that you know are going online one after another, yet you are not able to figure out if and how to do the same for your own business? Or perhaps, you have seen that everyday new Online Businesses come to exist and enter the market, creating a position for themselves and affecting the business of other players – mostly traditional ones - and of yours negatively?

Have you ever been overwhelmed by multiple software and solutions you are offered, when you wanted to build an Online Business or bring your existing Business, Online, not knowing which one is the right one for you and your business? Or perhaps, you have thought that your peers and competitors are mastering the world of Online Business better than you do, and hence moving faster in shaping their online business and as a result, the money is just flowing into their businesses? At the same time, you sit and doubt, if an online business is actually something for you, and your business and if you will ever be really making money by going online.

What if you could take your expertise and business ideas and shape them into your first Online Business? What if you could use state of the art, but readily available strategies and solution to transform your existing entity into a fast-growing and profitable online business? What if you could shape the next 'big thing 'in the company you work for? You have gotten innovative business ideas, a great vision, and long experience as an entrepreneur or intrapreneur. You have gotten knowledge, network, and know-how. And now, you want to transform them into an online machine serving your existing or future customers and your stakeholders while bringing you, prosperity, and profits.

If you are like most experienced and successful entrepreneurs or intrapreneurs, at a certain point wanting to grow your business further, but doubting if an online business is actually something for you, and your business; and if you are ever going to really make money by going online, I have good news for you!

You are not alone!

According to neuroscientist Jaak Panksepp, to be truly happy, you will always need something more. That is why humanity has been growing to this sophisticated physical, virtual, and societal complex system as we see today. That is why, exactly you successful entrepreneur or intrapreneur who has created the business to its current level, experience dissatisfaction and are the ones wanting more! More for themselves, their families, their employees, their customers, their society, and for the world. It is this desire for more which did result in all the inventions and enterprises we use and rely on today. And you find bringing your business Online, as the most important next step towards your ambitions.

I should tell you that you are in the right place. This book is designed to **step by step** help you in Ideating, Building, and Growing your successful Online Business from scratch or in Bringing your existing business Online. You can also use the strategies and techniques in this book to improve your already online business and bring it to its next level, increasing its revenue, profits, and impact. You can use this book as a self-implementation guide where you learn and get hints on strategies and solutions which you can implement yourself. You can also use this book as a guide in shaping your online strategy while asking your team or external partners to do the implementation for you. Hence, if you are a solo entrepreneur and want to do the work yourself or you are running a small or medium-size business wanting to design a roadmap which you will then ask for assistance from others in implementing it, in both these cases, you can massively benefit from this book. This book will give you the basic knowledge you need to build your online business, either when doing it yourself or having someone else building it for you.

I have also designed this book having the implementation of the recommendations in mind. Hence throughout the book, you will see multiple **Act Now** sections which will remind you of the actionable parts in which you need to roll up your sleeves and take action or ask your employees, partners, and suppliers to define and implement that action together with you.

One more thing! This is a **dynamic book**. By purchasing this book, you have also gotten access to all its future updates which I may create once in a while. I will add content, review, and update the existing ones and provide more strategies and techniques over time. All this will be at your reach, at no additional cost! This book comes also with a companion course. During reading the book, you will see references to the content sitting in the companion course. To access the course contents, the companion workbook, and to be able to benefit from all future updates and enhancements of this book, remember to register your book by signing up for the companion course.

Although we will start from the basics, but the way this book has been structured, makes it useful both for people who have an existing business with no online presence yet or those with a level of online business who want to improve or get a better grip of their processes and systems. The strategies and solutions offered in this book will help you put processes in place with which you can both grow and increase the efficiency of your business, resulting in more sales, profits, and higher impact. Moreover, although I have authored this book with solo entrepreneurs as well as small and medium companies (SMEs) in mind, the strategies and solutions offered are applicable to businesses of any size who want to go online. Hence join me, follow the steps, and enjoy the journey.

Act Now:

Download your copy of "Roadmap to Build an Online Business in 24 Hours" Workbook in the Course Downloads section of the companion course. Take a print or save a copy of it on your device. Go to the first page and answer some of these questions which are relevant to your circumstances, in a few bullet points. This exercise aims to create a high-level helicopter view of your intentions with building an online business, before you dig down into the details. Ask yourself, what are your reflections from reading the above introduction? Do you have thoughts on how to build an online business or bring your existing business online? Have you been exploring the most accessible ways and solutions to Build an Online Business? What is your mission for your existing or future intended business? What problem(s) are you trying to solve? What is functioning well in your existing business? What are the things you need improvement in? If you are starting a new business altogether, write down what comes to your mind when you think about where you will be in a year from now? What are the challenges in front? It is vital to write down and also to do it now. This is to ensure you capture your ideas and thoughts at the right stages and moments as you go through this book to maximize the benefit of the time you are spending. Be concise. But capture your thoughts into these bullet points so that you can remember and recall them when reading your notes later, as clear as you do now when you were thinking about and writing them down.

Build an Online Business Now

Let us first look at why it is the exact right time to start an Online Business Now. You may have a successful business that has been growing for years and is today in decent shape. You may also have a business that has been growing to some extent for a few years but struggling to go to its next level for some time. You may also have a business that has been struggling all the years since you have owned it. You may have experienced the impact of the crisis such as the economic downturn of 2008 or the corona pandemic of 2020 – which is around us as I am writing these sentences - challenging the existence of your business to the level you doubted its feasibility going forward. In all these scenarios, there is **one thing** you should look at carefully.

You may not have any online business or any business at all. Or you may have part of your business Online. Perhaps, this part is not really the successful part of your business, and lately, you have doubted if it is worth all the efforts you and your team have put into it. Or perhaps, you see your competitors benefiting from their online businesses much more than you do. The right question is not if the online part of your business is worth the effort. **The real question** is how you should benefit from your existing or future Online Business, making it contribute to most, if not all your sales and profits.

Online Business is an arm of your business which can enable you in diverse ways. On one hand, Online Business can contribute to a considerable part of your sales as its main or significant channel. On the other hand, Online Business can enable you grow your business without necessarily increasing your cost base proportionally. Imagine this. If you have a shop, you can grow your business in that single shop. But there is a level of sales beyond which you need to spend a lot of time and money to grow your sales and customer base. What can you do next? You may start to wonder why I do not open a second shop on the other side of the city? The point is, by running an online business, you may be able to serve the customers of the other side of the city, just through your web-shop and not necessarily by investing an enormous amount of money and time in creating a parallel operation next to what you already have. You may still want to open that second branch for whatever reason. But that will then be your choice, after proper considerations of all your options, online and offline. For example, a barbershop may well need to think of a second branch in this scenario, as your potential customers may not want to commute all the way to the other end of the city to have a haircut by you. At the same time, an architecture or law firm may well benefit from investing a fraction of the investment for a second office into a web presence solution enabling them to bring customers from across the town to their office or serve them remotely through their online business.

Online Businesses have also other benefits. As I write these sentences, we are in times in which you may have been noticing something as you walked through the empty streets of your city. Yes, a lot of stores have been closing down, and some forever. Closing stores are not the phenomenon of the last three to four months since the emergence of the recent crisis. This we have all been seeing for years. But what is happening now is that many of these stores who were doubting, if they should continue or not, are becoming sure of not. Their problem has just got multiplied by a factor of ten or more. You may yourself own such a business in need of thinking about its future. The impact of the crisis is much closer than we may imagine.

While experiencing these tough times, you also see incredibly significant growth on the eCommerce globally. Over the last few years, eCommerce has been growing between 10 to 16% year on year according to different researches, and this trend is going to just increase to a number which is more than 20% towards 2023. And these forecasts are all done before the 2020 global crisis. According to the latest researches, even in the most conservative forecasts, global eCommerce is going to take a much more significant share in the economy than before this crisis. World Economic Forum has also been publishing studies on additional benefits from eCommerce, including how the growth in eCommerce will result in more inclusive economies across the globe, including the less privileged parts giving additional reasons for it to grow.

Let us look at some other examples. You see, airlines are going bankrupt due to the current crisis, but then you also remember that some of these airlines were already in trouble even before all this crisis hit us. On the other hand, you see industries like Online Gaming growing by 10% year on year to become a $79 billion industry by 2025. You see cultural events, such as concerts and theatre shows, technology or political conferences, all sorts of events getting postponed or cancelled altogether. On the other side, you see that video conferencing industry is booming as it is used by more people and even more by the existing users. Video conferencing is going to grow by 20% year on year to become a $50 billion industry by 2026.

In June 2020, we heard about Apple becoming the first company in the world to hit one and a half-trillion dollars of market cap. Think about it: one and a half trillion market cap. And as you look to other big tech companies, they are not that different. They are in the race to hit One, One and a half and soon Two trillion dollars. And what is enabling them to do so? Yes, It is all the consumers and businesses using their devices and services as they go increasingly online. Some of us may like or dislike what we see, but the facts are on the table. And as a Businessperson, you should be focusing on facts.

Let us look at the online education market. The online education market has been growing by 24% since 2016 and is going to continue to do so towards 2023. And this is only a forecast done before the recent crisis. Now, the online education market is going to grow even further as even schools, universities and world-famous international conferences are seeing that there is no other way than joining the global trends and moving on with online education to retain their operations and to become resilient – and even to stay relevant - during and after the difficult times.

From one side, you see closed restaurants and all the other hospitality industry suffering because of the current crisis. From another side, you see all sorts of home delivery services from not only fast food, but also more decent restaurants are coming onto the market. Even the ones who were reluctant to jump onto this train learnt that there is no other way. They need to move onto this train and start to render their services online. Otherwise, there is some revenue at a certain period and perhaps no revenue during the next crisis. These businesses can simply not withstand another potential crisis on the horizon. Some of these businesses are even being closed at this moment without being able to live through the current crisis, let alone the next one.

Okay. You sit and look at Apple, you look at Amazon, you look at restaurants, you look at coffee shops, you look at the big giants and so on. Now you may ask, ok, I see all these facts. I see all the tech giants benefitting from their Online Businesses. I see also that the offline businesses are suffering more during tough times. But is an online business really going to help my company and me as well? What about a really small size business like mine? I am running a small shop in a corner or a medium-size company. You wonder, 'what are my options? Can I afford to bring my business online? Is it the right time to invest money in going online while being in the current difficult situation? And is that time really now?'

The answer to all above is a big yes. You might be someone who is trying to build an online business. You might also be someone who is trying to shape a new business from scratch. Why not think about bringing it completely, or at least partially online benefitting from tens of different values that the online world will bring with it. Some of the others reading this, having an existing business, you may want to safeguard your business during challenging times and make much more benefit during better times. In all these cases, you SHOULD **BUILD A ROBUST ONLINE BUSINESS NOW**. That is the **one thing** you should look at carefully and how to do it to create more sales, profits and impact is **the real question** you should find an answer to.

Your business is not something like a Computer program that, if it did not respond, you can close and open a new instance of it again. You need to take care of your business, expand, and enhance it all the time. You also need to protect your existing business in difficult times. And You need to reduce costs at all times, primarily for the benefit of your customers. Especially the costs such as the cost of sales or other administration and support processes costs which are not what the customer is really willing to pay for. There is also so much of competition in almost any sector you can imagine. That is why the cost of sales is increasing enormously, and you need to reduce it along with other none-value-adding cost elements. You need also to be able to invest in new equipment and tools, in your people, in new products, in your existing facility, in the infrastructure you have, in new software, and most importantly in yourself. And you need to have the money to make these investments. Hence it is vital to release money from what you have been spending it on and invest it in what matters. **Online Business enables you to reduce your cost base** and release your money to invest in what really matters.

You want returning customers who purchase more than once and hopefully frequently as the returning customers, do not need the same amount of efforts in order to be sold to; which means that you will reduce your cost of sales, not to zero, but considerably lower amounts compared to the ones for new customers. **Online Businesses offer wonderful ways to create returning customers.**

On the other hand, you need to have the **predictability of your business** and not only in these challenging times. You need also to have that predictability in regular times to be able to understand what you should expect as the volume of your business next month, the month after; and as an outcome, how you should plan for it; how many people you need; how much ingredients you need; how much resources you need; what will your cost levels be and so on. And in the end, you need to leave through downturns and crises like the ones we experienced in 2020, which is a particularly important reason also to consider, to bring your business online.

You might also be reading this book being among the ones not yet having any business altogether, thinking about all the possibilities of the Online Businesses, saying yeah, maybe I should also become an online entrepreneur. You are probably someone who has been thinking for years to start a business for yourself. You are wondering if a new business is a source of **additional income**, or if it will bring **more choices** for you and makes you able to stay open for new opportunities. The point is that if you start a new business without considering the potential of today's online world, you are going to lock yourself into a traditional business, hence soon realizing you actually do not have a business! There is a business with one employee in it. And that employee happens to be you. You are the employee of your own business doing all the needed with your own hands in a traditional way. And the only way to get out of this situation is to think, to enable your business by **automation, outsourcing** to people and other companies. Online Businesses make all this both possible and easier. In summary, if you are wondering about becoming an entrepreneur, you need to think seriously about online business and the potential it creates for your future business, before embarking on any business idea.

A mistake that most entrepreneurs do is to use the business knowledge which is decades old. The decades-old best practices of business told us to outsource. Outsourcing was a way to increase efficiency, reduce costs, and focus on the core. Today, there is a small yet extremely critical change you need to consider in this practice. Before going to the expensive solution of outsourcing to people and other companies who have the mission to maximize their value capture, it is important to automate and to automate more. You need to make things digital and to go online to be able to automate as much as possible; whatever left, which is not possible to be digitalized, may be outsourced.

Yes, irrespective of being a professional entrepreneur, a new-bee, or a to-be-preneur, or being an intrapreneur in the corporate world, creating an Online Business is a solid choice for your and your company! And there is no better time than NOW given all the reasons explained above.

Act Now:

Go back to your workbook "Roadmap to Build an Online Business in 24 Hours" downloaded from the Course Downloads section of the companion course. On page 4, write down what you have learned in this section in two sentences. Write down also if you have a decision for yourself or for your business that you made as you read this section. Or if you had a decision lingering in your mind, and now you are sure you have taken it and are committed to making it happen. Look at your first exercise you did before as well. Are there any points that you want to change, given your new thoughts from reading this last section? You can always come back and revise what you have written for this section as you learn, and as you mature your idea and the approach in creating your online business.

What is better than a crisis?

It is probably sad, but many of the successes of the human being has been coming out of a big crisis. It was once said that nothing could be a better gift to a business than a good crisis. Why? First of all, during a crisis, we have changing equations. What is happening to the old players? Some of them are starting not to be as strong and confident as they were before. What does that mean? It means some of them will be looking for ways to get back onto their feet and start to act with the performance they had before. This is a business opportunity. For whom? For those business consultants who want to help these companies to come back onto their feet; because otherwise and if these companies do not come back to normal operations, the processes and the infrastructure of our societies are going to stop functioning.

Some other businesses are not going to be able to come back. They have probably been struggling already for months or years in order to have a prosperous business. And now, with this added push by the crisis, their business is simply not feasible anymore. What does that mean? It means there is another business opportunity. If these companies have been in a serious business, they should have been producing products or delivering services that customers buy and use. Think of food, clothes, energy, beauty and hygiene, dining, entertainment, consumer electronics, and many more. Or perhaps they have been supporting other businesses with their hardware, software, logistics, administration, or any other services. All these services need to continue to exist. Of course, a crisis can and will change people's consumption and buying patterns and behavior. But as you come out of such a crisis, some of the basic services need to go back to the level that they have been before, if not becoming more or better. And when some of these businesses are not able to come back, it simply means that we are going to see opportunity space in the market. For whom? For some other people, entrepreneurs who will grab the opportunity and start serving those customers who are left without their suppliers, the supermarkets, the restaurants, the shops, the food suppliers, the engineering companies, the law firms, the administration services and you name it.

That is how opportunity spaces are shaped. It is not always that an innovative technology or some smart business idea brings new opportunities. It is sometimes the crisis, which brings these opportunity spaces. It is important now to investigate what type of opportunities this crisis – or one we may face in future - is giving us.

Last but not least is the 'new-new'. New-new is something which did not exist yesterday. You may think of smartphones. We had mobile phones; there were no smartphones. And somehow somebody thought it would be good to have a mini PC in the palm of your hand doing much more than calling and texting with it. And that vision resulted in having a different type of products, maturing one after another. And then the technology came to help in bringing the smartphones to a level that the advanced smartphones of today are more potent than the mainframes and servers of a ministry a few decades ago. This progress has not started because of technology;

the technology that was used to build the first smartphone did also exist a couple of years before that, but the vision of somebody for something completely new, brought the smartphones where they are today. Looking into a new need, which did not exist in the market, created this opportunity. It is about giving people something they did not think they wanted before it existed. How this crisis is going to inspire entrepreneurs to make products or services people will love which they did not know they wanted them so badly?

Act Now:

Go back to your workbook "Roadmap to Build an Online Business in 24 Hours" downloaded from the Course Downloads section of the companion course. On page 5, write down what has been the last crisis that hit you or your business. What are the pains that the crisis has caused you, your family, your network, your business, your customers, and your competitors? What has moved in the market? What has not moved for a long period? What were the permanent changes? What do these changes in the past or recent mean to you and your business? What are the threats of these changes to your existing or future business? Is there any opportunity in this situation for you? Think of changing needs in the market. Think of changed equations where some companies did need help to get back onto their feet. Think of the ones who did not manage or will not manage to come back. Think of changes in people's and businesses ' consumption and buying patterns. This exercise will help you move from envisioning, to defining a real market demand, being it, an existing or a future demand. It is important to go through this exercise to ensure you have a robust business idea for whose products and services, there are people who want to pay.

Discovering your golden opportunity

When you experience a crisis or simply when you find an unsatisfied need in the market, you should think about it in three different layers. Think about changing equations and how that is affecting the market with some businesses able to come back, but needing help. Consultants! Jump on it! Think about the second level of businesses who are not able to come back and will not be able to come back even later. Can you serve their customers? This is the second opportunity. Businesspeople! Go for it! And the third, look into what people want today or will want tomorrow when we are out of the crisis. Start shaping that service or product now and deliver it to them before they even ask for it. Entrepreneurs and Intrapreneurs! Take it on! This might sound too easy, but that is the recipe for the success of entrepreneurs, not only in tough times but throughout the history of entrepreneurship. In contrast, they are those who doubt and keep asking the questions until the window of opportunity is closed, and the temporarily changing equations in the market are stabilized as new players as well as traditional players who have adjusted themselves and their businesses, have taken the opportunity spaces created in the market. Are you among the ones **asking** or the ones **answering**?

Act Now:

Go back to your workbook "Roadmap to Build an Online Business in 24 Hours" downloaded from the Course Downloads section of the companion course. On page 6 and write down the moving equations in the market. What are those movements? Is that giving you an opportunity space? Look into your notes so far. Is there anything missing? Can you think of any need in the market in any of the three layers? Can you help companies who are facing challenges to get back onto their feet? Are there needs not temporarily satisfied by old players? Can you do something there? Is there a possibility to enter the market and do something different using a new mindset and method? And are there areas where you can define a new product or service fit for people as the world is emerging out of the crisis or as people are becoming open to new solutions in different domains? Think of "the smartphone of your industry" if your industry is producing something like the old mobile phones at this moment. Can you introduce that 'smartphone'? This is a key step to bring your business idea to become a specific product or service which you will sell to your future customers.

Shape and Grow a Prosperous Business

Throughout my life, I have always been fascinated by technology and its contribution to shaping and developing our societies and humanity to what it is today. I have started exploring the world of technology and touching software programing since the age of 12. I have been experiencing entrepreneurship at the age of 22 and since then have been into different senior leadership positions in the corporate world at the international level, engaging with businesses and customers on one side and the technology and software from another side. In all these years, I have seen how limited the knowledge of some of the entrepreneurs and intrapreneurs on the possibilities of simple but robust solutions for the online presence of their businesses is. I have also seen how lack of agility has been hindering the creation of genuine business value through digitalization efforts. I have also been seeing smaller companies considering quitting as the only option in the though times. Hence, I have written this book as an attempt to inspire and assist some of those entrepreneurs and intrapreneurs.

You invest a few hours of your valuable time reading this book. By the time you come to the end of it, you have already established the basics of your online presence by thinking about how to bring your Online Business Ideas onto paper and make sense of them, how to design and create your Online Business and how to build this business using the strategies and solutions you learn throughout the book. You will literally spend 24 hours to complete your work and Go Online if you wish so. You can also choose to go step by step and use the book as a user manual – or your digital consultant – walking you through the steps you need to take in order to go online.

Can you do this? If you can follow the recommended steps, I don't see why not. When needed, I even go right down to what software you may use or where you should look at. And then, you always have the possibility to post your questions on my website (link in at the end of the book). I will try to provide answers to these questions in my articles or other content on the website. This book is created to be the game plan for Entrepreneurs who want to Go Online in 24 Hours without wasting months or even years in doubt or trial and error the way to success. Unlike some other books and courses that take a more conceptual or complicated approach towards online businesses build and digitalization, this book is written for the Entrepreneurs who want to shape or improve their online presence now and enhance their sales, profits and impact from their online business from day one.

"Build an Online Business In 24 Hours" is created to handhold you, providing you with all the strategies that have worked for many before you. Do start building your online business as you go through the chapters of the book. You can literally come out of reading this book with your business, online, and all its online components set up and launched. You will come out of this book having your website live, social media channels set up and integrated into your online business. You will have your payment gateways set and ready to go, and you will have your online shop selling your products and service for you. Just go and make money by creating a positive impact in people's lives!

Putting skin into the game

Yes, building an online business is simple, but it is not going to necessarily be easy. Why? Because not all are ready to take action. We always have three choices. We can do something today, or we can also postpone it to tomorrow. There is a third way, and that is to Act 'Now'. To create a successful business, including an online one, today is late. It is this leaving the action for today – which frequently slips to tomorrow – which results in many businesses conceptualizing and dreaming their online businesses for years instead of Acting Now. If you act now, it is this commitment and agility, which will change your priorities and increase the productivity level that you will gain and need to carry throughout the journey to achieve results. It is simply the procrastination from now to today and from today to tomorrow, which keeps entrepreneurs and enterprises stay still and do not move on simply wait for the right time to take action or wait until that next study on the impact of digitalization on their business is completed. My commitment to you is to provide you with valuable information, simple strategies, and affordable solutions in creating an online business. Your responsibility will be to understand, evaluate, and use them to build or transform the online business of your dream Now. Think about what type of actions you are going to take after you have finished this book.

Act Now:

Go back to your workbook "Roadmap to Build an Online Business in 24 Hours" downloaded from the Course Downloads section of the companion course. On page 7, write down how will you ensure your and your organization's commitment to build an online business in 24 Hours. You can spend the needed 24 hours over a weekend or split it over more sessions, like 12 sessions of 2 hours each. But you must commit to the outcome and the plan that you put down here. That is the skin you should put into the game. As you read through this book, you will come back and adjust your plans and timelines. But the commitment needs to stay firm. The simple reason that, for example, you not knowing how to digitalize a process yet, should not result in reducing the scope of your online journey from your original intentions. You should instead search more and ask the experts for advice on how to benefit from unknown (to you) yet existing solutions (to some of your competitors) to achieve more significant results. This exercise intends to ensure you create commitment and plans to build your envisioned online business to deliver the products and services you have thought of in the earlier exercise.

How Much Online Can it be?

Now comes the real question. I call this the Golden Question you should ask. I hope and am sure you will take a lot with you from reading and implementing the actions from this book. But if not, bring this one question with you and ask it again and again. Ask this question when thinking of building a new (online) business. Ask it when thinking of changing certain parts of your existing business using some online software and solutions. Ask it when you want to consider if your whole business can be digitalized or perhaps replaced by a software doing all the work you and your team do for your customers so that you almost become a software company than what you are now.

Let me then put it clearly and in bold for you.

"How much online can it be?"

Feel free to replace 'be 'with 'become 'if you are considering this for your existing business, which has no or some level of digitalization and hence online components. Feel also free to have different iterations of this question and try to answer those as well. Stretch your alternative questions to the limits of your imagination until it becomes difficult to believe there would be a solution and answer to them. It is through these multiple questions and seeking answers to them, that you will realize what is possible that you did not know or could not imagine.

The rest of this book will mostly be spent exactly on answering these type of questions. But before we continue, let me use this section to give you some examples which can clarify the importance of these questions, and also the depth of the answers and almost unbelievable solutions [for none-IT people] you can find for them. Hence, let me try to answer to few iterations of this question in brief.

How much online can it be? Very much, perhaps totally. An iteration of this question has been asked by Forbes magazine while they have tried to find an answer to a question. Remember the law firm example from chapter 1?. Forbes tried to ask "Will Artificial Intelligence Put Lawyers Out of Business?" This is the question. What do you think it is asking? Is it basically asking how much online a legal service can become? Is it that it is the website of the law firm giving access to some useful information and maybe a library or link to some of the national or international laws and also contact information for their offices enriching their customers 'experience in interacting with them? Or can it also be an online booking system that customers can use to book their appointments with the lawyers without needing to call their offices to improve the quality and efficiency of the scheduling process? Can it be that some of the documents are sent in a secure environment for pre-reading by the lawyers, saving time from both them as well as their clients before their first face to face meeting? Can it be that the face to face meeting is replaced by a Skype, FaceTime, or Zoom call or something similar? No. The question is not any of these. Expand your imagination. The question is simply asking, can the whole law firm be replaced with a software doing even the advice and review of the legal documents on the spot and concluding in seconds in contrast to what a lawyer would do over few sessions of interacting with the customer and going through some steps manually. Can the law firm become a legal software firm?

You may not need or be yet able to fully digitalize neither a law firm nor your own business. But it is important to explore and find out the answer to this question. There are people who are against all this digitalization. They also have a point. But irrespective of our viewpoint, what can be digitalized, will probably be digitalized. Hence, instead of sitting on defense until you are wiped out of the market, better to roll up sleeves and play the game. I also have my reservations on some of the digitalization and their impact on our world. I will probably write an article and share my views and some of the opinions of other experts in this field on my website. But for this book, the idea is not to discuss philosophy. Let us stick to our agenda: the online business build.

How much and how fast can my business become online if I do not have even a website yet? In the past, creation of a website was almost equal to software programming; with a difference that regular software programs would sit on your hard disk and run on your computer, but the new software (i.e. the website) would sit on another computer – a server – and accessed through the Internet by your internet browser like Internet Explorer, Chrome, Firefox, Safari, and so on. But today, the designing of a website has become more like drawing a picture on your computer. You can draw a simple picture using a tool like the Paintbrush program. You can also draw a high-resolution piece of art and design some really professional content for the media using a software like Photoshop. If you want to create your simple website for your business, it may actually be that you need a simple tool to design your website as simple as

Paintbrush in creating a simple image. And there are tools like that available. You can literally build a website and have it up and running in less than one hour, having zero programming knowledge. There are, of course, more advanced tools. There are hundreds if not thousands of tools you can use, ranging from the simple tools to create a small website to a suite of different software and technologies to build a complicated website. It is up to you what to choose, and it all depends on your need. For most businesses, the basic website can be created in a matter of hours or a couple of days using easy to use – zero code – tools. You will learn about some of these tools in the next chapters.

Can I sell my products online? How much online can the process of selling my product or service become? This is another iteration of the same question. It basically is asking if my going online can go beyond having a website with few nice pages as well as some contact details, but to enable my customers actually to buy my products and services from the same website. You know the answer already as you probably yourself buy some of the products and services from time to time online. You are already doing Online Business. But the point is that you are the one who is paying. Not the one who is getting paid. That needs to change. Then comes the next question.

How much effort is it to create an online shop? How much does it take to create a functioning online web-shop? If you are a techie, you know the answer. But if not, let me tell you. You can learn to build an online web-shop in a matter of a few hours. Some may know this. But for most, it will be a major surprise. Let me repeat the answer. You can build a functioning web-shop if you want, in a matter of minutes or a couple of hours. You can always expand that and build much more functionality and sophistication into your webshop. But to be able to sell a product online, you need only a few hours to be ready to get your first customer purchasing from you.

Just as an example, imagine you have now created your product, or you already have one from your existing business. Imagine you have a shop selling something, or you have a restaurant, and you want to go online. Let us start with a straightforward example. Let us imagine you even do not have any product to sell.

Act Now:

Watch the YouTube video the "build a drop shipping business in 24 hours section" of the companion course. This young man has created a dropshipping business in 24 hours. Yes, you read it correctly. For those of you who do not know what dropshipping is, dropshipping is a way of selling other people's products. What you do is that you create an online page, even not a full website, simply a one-page website. And you start selling products which you source from someone else. It could be that it is your friends making something, or it could be that you find products from other companies where they are willing to give you the possibility to sell that product for them online, building such business. In this example, he has done everything you need to do and had even his first breakeven point within 24 hours.

See also the Additional Examples I have added - and will continue to add – to the first chapter in the companion course.

Creating a professional web-shop with all its programmed processes may not be a job of 24 hours, but what this gentleman has been trying to do is to show that, to set it up, you don't really need more than 24 hours. And when you watch this video, you will realize that he is starting to make money within the first 24 hours. Now you may think, okay, this is an attempt to take on a challenge as he did. But how much money is he actually making? Maybe couple of hundred dollars. You may say, but I am talking about serious businesses. I am talking about a shop, a company, or even an enterprise.

That is right. But that is exactly my point. The process of being able to build something or drive the change fast is not something that is dependent on the type of industry or the size of your business. It is exactly this mistake that prevents many businesses from going online and create success as they keep complicating things to the extent that they never act. Let me give you an example from a real business. In the companion course, you also see the example from a famous chocolate company which brought its business online during the covid-19 crisis in 5 days! Agility in business decisions and their implementation is a choice and not a gift given only to some. Let us look at an extremely different example from two hefty construction projects to describe how your approach to running a project can change the outcome irrespective of the scope of that project.

The logic of acting with agility can be applied also in a very non-digital offline business as well. These photos show the highway A4 in the Netherlands close to where I live. A large part of this highway has existed for years. But there was a small part in between not constructed, where there were farms and other pieces of land. A good portion of this part has now been built underground [see the photo showing the land above the road] as a tunnel or lower than the lands around [see the photo showing the road build slightly below the surface] to reduce the impact on lands and houses above. The process of negotiating with the communities and the political process, finalizing the route, necessary adjustments, the final detail design, and what you have, has been taking some time before they were able to build this section of the road and connect the two other existing sides to each other. How long do you think it took to complete this small part of the highway in between the two existing ends?

It's difficult to guess. Because the fact is that this has taken not less than half a century to build this part of the road! Like many other construction projects, from the beginning of saying, according to the national and provincial master plans, we have an intention to build a road and then to connect these two parts, building parts of it over the years, until the road was finally completed with this new section and became completely open to public traffic has taken actually more than sixty years. To see the actual photo and some more information about this project, please visit the Project Management section in chapter 1 of the companion course of this book.

This photo shows another project in another Dutch highway (Highway A17). As you can see in the photo, they have built a tunnel for the cars under this very busy highway. It is a major road, and there are thousands and thousands of cars and trucks passing this road every single day. By closing a road like this for a few months, you get big chaos and considerable damage to the economy. But then what should you do? You will come with this smart project plan to build this highway, not in many years. Of course, this is a much smaller project compared to the previous example. Maybe this one should take around a year or a bit less. But we cannot afford to close this road even for a year. Let us think of six months or perhaps three? Is that possible? The fact is that they have built this tunnel over one single weekend.

Yes. This has been taking a weekend to be built. To see the actual photo's and some more information about this, please visit the Project Management section in chapter 1 of the companion course of this book.

The point from mentioning these two examples is the following. You can think about the two above examples, considering what kind of frame conditions has resulted in each of them to be approached in a different way (progressive and robust, versus quick with lots of pre-planning). You can achieve the desired outcome in any kind of project in different ways. It is important to understand the scale of your project. Are you dealing with a complicated project (technically, commercially, socially, or business-wise) or a simple one? What are the applicable boundary conditions? For example: Do you want something nice enough, up and running tomorrow, or a robust system scalable for years which will take a few months to launch? What kind of budgets do you have? Who are your customers and other stakeholders? These are some of the components influencing the way you define and manage any project, including a project for an online business build.

Back to this question, **how fast can my business become online, or can I create a web-shop?** If an underpass under a busy highway can be built over a weekend, your website and web-shop should be built by the time you have finished imagining them ☺

Building an Online Business should not be a painful exercise. In fact, I find building online businesses like artwork. Entertaining and fun! And the outcome, something that is appreciated by you and your customers. In a more traditional business environment [mostly seen in the corporate world], you may need to take a different approach, more similar to the approach on building a highway in a progressive manner, to both manage the expectations of stakeholders, but also to distribute the much higher level of investments needed over a longer period of time. But in the smaller companies, that should not be the case.

The next question coming to your mind will probably be this one:

How can I get paid online? Or basically, how long does it take to create an online payment solution for my web-shop? You know the game by now. This will take literally 30 minutes max. You can complicate this to the level needed. But to create a "Merchant Account", connect your bank account to it, and link that merchant account to your web-shop or website, you need about 30 minutes of work.

Let me stop here. There are tens of similar questions you may have, and I would like to answer them all. But we have all the rest of the book to answer some of these questions. We will look into what is necessary to build an online business step-by-step and answer to potential questions you may have while going through each of those steps. Moreover, you can always post these types of questions on my website (link at the end of the book).

Act Now:

Go back to your workbook "Roadmap to Build an Online Business in 24 Hours" downloaded from the Course Downloads section of the companion course. On page 8, write down how much online do you want your business to be (or become)? What parts of it did you wish you could bring online? Is there any example you have seen that you can think of? Is there a competitor of yours, another website in your own or other industries or something totally different you have seen that is your aspiration for your future online business? Capture that in some bullet points concisely, but precisely so that you can recall your thoughts when you read it back later in the process we are following together. This exercise aims to set the first draft of your ambition for your future online business.

How Much Is It Going to Cost?

Knowing you being businesspeople, no topic is adequately addressed before also saying how much is it going to cost. Creating an Online Business is an investment. Hence it is quite up to you and your wishes and plans on how much to invest. For example, creating a simple website with a couple of pages by yourself may cost a few dollars per month in total. A more complicated website may still only cost a few hundred dollars while creating an overly complex website with lots of functionalities may be a project costing a few thousand dollars. It is the same for all other solutions in bringing your business online. You may create a web-shop with very little money. It will be functioning, and you can start making money online. But you may over time, want to make your web-shop more advanced and move it slowly to more robust platforms as your business grows and as you get more customers onboard. Hence, forget about thinking you will need a lot of money to bring your business online or to create an online business. It is usually quite affordable to create an online business even for an individual.

Moreover, since a decade, Cloud solutions have been heavily replacing traditional on-premise software. Cloud solutions are software installed on servers of their providers which remove the need to install software on your own premises and hence remove the need to have the infrastructure which was necessary in the past. Cloud solutions break the investment costs into quite affordable monthly fees. Hence, you will never need a big chunk of money to establish your online presence. You can start by a few dollars a month for a solo-entrepreneur or a couple of hundred dollars a month for more advanced solutions and for SMEs and scale up as you grow and make more profits. For example, there are solutions that you can use to start a web-shop selling your physical products, or to start teaching your skills online or do provide coaching and advisory. You may be able to start any such a business with almost no money upon start and in monthly fees of a hundred dollars or a bit more.

In short, the answer to how much is it going to cost depends on your plans and the size of your ambition but it is much more affordable than you may think and much less than what it used to be in the past.

Chapter 2 – The What

If you already know what kind of online business you want to start or you want to bring your existing business online, you may decide to skip this chapter and go straight to the next one. You can also decide to read this chapter to get the insights I share here, even if you are already clear on what kind of online business you want to start. But what if you do not have any business idea, but still want to start an online business? This is what I will cover in this chapter.

What If You Do Not Have Any Business Idea?

The process to decide what business to start is a separate subject in itself, which I will cover in my future publications. But I have added a condensed version of such a publication in this chapter to help people who have an interest in starting an online business, yet not sure what business they actually want to start.

To start any business, including an online one, you need to answer few questions. Who are your customers? What do they need or want? What are you going to deliver to them as product or service which will answer to their needs, or are you perhaps able to provide them with something they did not think themselves, they needed, which they will love after they got to know it existed? What does it take to make that product or prepare to be able to deliver that service? Are you able to do that alone, or you want some others (suppliers) to provide you with some ingredients or components you need in making that product or service? Are there any equipments or tools necessary? Think of both physical equipment and tools like machinery, but also virtual tools like software and processes. How much is all this going to cost? How many instances of the product or service do you foresee you will be able to sell? What is the price your customers are willing to pay? Have you done some research verifying the answers you give to all the above questions especially the last three? Is your income (fees times price) more than your cost (sum of all cost elements you have thought of)? Are you left with any profits? What kind of things can go wrong? Think of issues in the market, with producing products, with the services and ingredients you get from suppliers, and so on. What would happen in each of those cases? Think of what you would do in each case. What about the market? Are there existing players producing comparable products and services that will be your future competitors? Be critical here. Be so clear on why you will be better than them. It is not about being the only one in the market. It is about finding a **relative competitive advantage** which enables you to find your customers in a market along with those other players.

Act Now:

Go back to your workbook "Roadmap to Build an Online Business in 24 Hours" downloaded from the Course Downloads section of the companion course, page 9. Try to capture the answers to the questions on this page as clear as possible. Be concise. This helps you to be clear. Instead of expressing your answers in long sentences, stick to a few words and bullet points that best describe the answer to each of these questions. If you are not really clear about your answers to some of these questions, do not be disappointed by yourself. We will continue improving your answers during the next steps in this chapter. The intention of this exercise is to see what it would really take to build a business to make the products and services you intend to deliver.

The If and The What

The decision 'if start a business' and actually 'what business to start' are intertwined. You could be spending days, weeks, and even months, planning and shaping the business you have decided to start. But at a certain point, you may get the feeling that you are not progressing as you wished, and even worse, you may start to doubt if this is the right business to start or if it is the right one at this moment. One of the main reasons for the slow progress is this doubt on what business to start. Yes. This question keeps coming back even when you are in the very mature stages of setting up your business. Apart from serial entrepreneurs, the rest of the people tend to think once, then twice and then thrice and so on instead of just starting what they have decided to do.

One of the means to overcome this challenge is that early in your thought process know which different possibilities you have. What types of business can you start, and what are the chances of you succeeding in any of these potential businesses? After such a thought process reflecting on your possibilities in a structured manner, you will land on a decision which is firmer than before you did this exercise. Then you stick to that decision unless you find a better one during your exploration. Let us see how this process may in practice look like.

What Are Your Options

This is a question that you may have asked yourself, especially if you throughout your career have been employed or been having one single business you owned all the time. This is how the question of 'what are my options' comes to your mind when you want to start your first ever or next business.

Act Now:

Go back to the Course Downloads section of the companion course and download the "Business Ideation Worksheet" or save a copy of it on your device. Use this file to capture your thoughts as we go through the few upcoming sections of this chapter.

Your Product or Service

To try to find out what business you should start, think about these questions: Is there any specific product that you have or can get access to? Is there an evolution of an existing product which can be your product? Do people come to you for advice? What advice do people come to you for? What is the current Job you have? Do you have a passion for something which is either your own job or a hobby on the side? Go to your past and list all things you are or once have been good at? Will someone pay for that? Think if someone would love to learn those skills from you? Think if you can make those skills into a product or an experience that can be delivered to those asking for it. What about the history of all the different work that you have done before your current profession? Do you have a personal resume? Get a copy of that in hand and try to go through it up and down to find out if there is something which you have not been mentioning on your CV. Add those and use all those, even the small ones you have done for a month or two, to create a full list of all your skills and experience. Have you done any volunteer work? Add that as well.

Now see if you find an area which stands out. Stands out either because you have a passion and desire to work in that area or stands out because you hear a lot of demand in the market for that skill or product. The crucial point is to find one which has both sides, your passion, and the market demand for it.

Do not ignore anything at this stage. Even something less interesting for you as you go through your ideas can become what you at the end want to focus on during your process. Hence, list all the ideas before starting to kick some out and arrive at your shortlist. And if you do not have much on the list, do not be disappointed in yourself. Continue the process until the end, and I promise you, your list will not be empty at all.

Products and Services of Others

You may not have any products or services, or you may not be able to think of one after all the process you have gone through in the previous section. An alternative to selling your products or services is to sell other people's products or services! That is quite simple to understand. But yet not many think of this as a wonderful way to start your own business, including an online business.

Think of some of the most successful businesses in the world with different scales. The grocery shops are perhaps the most visited shops in the world. They are the ones who stay open during holidays and weekends and even during a crisis. What do they sell? Other people's products! Now think of any shop which is not producing the product itself. This applies to most of the shops apart from the bakery baking self, or restaurants, and so on. In most of cases, a shop is a trading entity than a production facility. What can be an online version of a shop? Bingo! A Web-shop!

Now think of a larger size example. Have you ever used websites like Booking.com, Expedia, Airbnb, and so on? What do they do? They sell other people's services i.e. hotel rooms, plane tickets, travel packages, and so on. Think of companies like Uber or Lyft. What do they sell? Drivers' riding services. Think of websites like LinkedIn Learning or Udemy. What do they sell? Other people's training courses.

Selling other people's products is not only for smaller or larger companies. It is for both. People want access to products and services, and if you can give them that access – and convenience –

they are willing to purchase from you. You may think I do not have a shop to sell other people's products. Or I do not have a website to sell other people's products online. And even if so, how do I find products that the producer or the seller may want me to sell for them. There is an answer to all these questions. And implementing those answers are not difficult. Have you heard of phrases like Affiliate marketing or Drop-shipping? These are what the online world makes possible. To learn more, go to the next section.

Affiliate programs

An affiliate program is performance-based marketing in which a business rewards one or more affiliates for each visitor or customer brought by the affiliate's own marketing efforts (Wikipedia). Affiliate programs are more common than you can think of. There are a lot of companies looking for more customers. And to achieve that, they not only build their in-house marketing teams but also benefit from external marketers, including professional marketing agents as well as an amateur or experienced individuals as their affiliates. The more you learn and explore this domain, the more you will discover affiliate programs that you did not know existed. You will find ways to distinguish the more favorable ones considering their referral fees and other terms and conditions. If you want to learn more about affiliate programs, how they work, and how you can find one or more that is suitable for you and your business, visit the Growth strategies section in the chapter 2 of the companion course.

Drop-shipping

As mentioned in chapter 1, Drop-shipping is a way of selling other people's products. What you do is that you create a simple website and start selling products, which you source from someone else. There are thousands of companies and millions of products you can find who can become part of your product and service portfolio without you sometimes even seeing these products! In most of the drop-shipping arrangements, the company producing these products will be sending the product directly to your customer after you have sold that product to them online. This removes all the challenges of production and logistics for you, leaving you with a profit margin because of the sales efforts you (or your website) have put in place. To find out more about drop-shipping products and the ways you can set up a drop-shipping business, visit the Growth strategies section in the chapter 2 of the companion course.

Act Now:

Go back to the Course Downloads section of the companion course and download the "Business Ideation Worksheet" or save a copy of it on your device. Use this file to capture both your ideas about what you may be able to make (either products or services or both) and sell online as well as possible products you may want to source from others and sell it on your website. See the links in the companion course for inspiration of what you could in your affiliate or drop-shipping business sell.

Growing Your Business

It may sound obvious. But growing your existing business is a business strategy that most people do easily forget. Although this chapter is about people without any business idea, but I still do write this section to remind to both existing as well as future entrepreneurs that one of the best ways to build a business, including an online one, may be to grow your own business, using online channels and tools.

The reason why this strategy works is the following. Many of the business owners, including the successful ones have been finding and following the tactics which made them successful over the years. They have shaped a great customer base using their sales and customer relation skills. They have improved their offerings by keeping a high quality of products and services. They have done great marketing campaigns creating a flow of new customers. They have learned their competitors well, knowing their strengths and weaknesses to use them to their favor. They have improved their processes to bring their cost down while keeping the efficiency and quality at an appropriate level. They may even have been branching out to other sectors or opening new branches of their business in the same sector in other districts, other cities, or countries.

What successful entrepreneurs may not have been realizing is that even all this success might have been possible with either less efforts – i.e. less cost – or with more impact – i.e. more sales and revenue.

Growing your own business is not only a process you continuously run but is a strategy you must consciously choose. And when you choose it strategically, it can become a basis on how you establish or transform your existing business.

Let me give you an example. Imagine you run a hair salon. You have been successful over many years, building this business from scratch. Now you are famous, you have regular customers, and you get a good flow of new customers growing your business continuously and taking care of the customers you lose as they relocate or change their salon. Over the years, there has been a slow change in the business environment and market dynamics. Not that much that you have even realized. But now that you think it is more difficult to run this business than it was a decade ago. You may have new relations with your employees. Some of them now are not paid by you, but they are running their chair. You get some monthly fees or a percentage of their earnings. For some others, you have them as employees. You deal with their salaries, taxes, social security, and pension. On the customer side, there are newer generation of customers with new expectations and new relations. There are also more hair salons out there. Moreover, some other businesses, like the ones previously providing only skincare services, have also started with hair-related services. To keep up with all these changes, you need to do a lot by refurbishing your shop, doing some advertisements in the papers or on local websites, starting to sell some hair products on your shelf and more.

On the other hand, you could implement other types of actions you have not considered before. Have you been working enough on your brand? If not, what could be the outcome of doing that? Could you decide on a growth strategy for your business that does not need you to work more hours and spend more money than already increased amounts of both you spend these days? What could that be? There are many answers to this question. Here I share one. Think of making your brand so famous that one other hair salon in another side of the city may want so much to compete with you that they hate you. What if you go to that business owner and offer them to use your brand? What do you do then? You ask him or her to adjust the shop with colors and look and feel, which is similar to yours and to adjust the brand. Now you have a franchise business! You get a percentage of his income or a fixed monthly fee because you have been enabling him or her to benefit from your greatly established brand. You perhaps can also ask the same from a new entrepreneur who wants to start a hair salon to go for becoming your franchise than starting with its own brand and settings. You can also do the same with one of your best employees who has been thinking of starting for its own. If you do this well, you create a win-win situation for yourself and your first franchise partner!

This is an example of a growth strategy compared to traditional growth. There are tens of different ways you can think of growing your business as a new business idea. Want to learn more? Visit the Growth strategies section in the chapter 2 of *the companion course*.

Grow Businesses of Others

If you cannot think of your products and services or did not manage to choose to sell other people's products yet, or you do not have a business or a growth strategy for your existing business, you can still start a business. Another way to build a business is to help others grow their businesses. Assisting other people to grow their businesses can bring you income through getting paid per lead you bring to them, or by getting a percentage of the sales or profits they make. In other situations, you may also be able to get equity in the business of your customers as a reward in helping them grow the business. Or perhaps you can help others in their marketing strategy, marketing campaigns, and in managing their social media with the focus on generating leads and sales. Hence learning the skills on how to build a business including an online one, is not only helpful for you when you own that business, but can also create another type of business which is advisory or partnership relations resulting in increased sales and profits which your customers share with you using one of the models above. Want to learn more about how you can find opportunities to help others grow their business? Visit the Growth strategies section in the chapter 2 of *the companion course*.

Online Courses

For some, this is such an obvious option. For others, it is a big surprise asking, "I have never been a teacher. Why do you think I can teach something? Let alone make money from teaching and even doing so online!". Each individual has knowledge and skills about certain things because of his or her educational background, work experience, hobbies, or other experiences throughout life. Hence, Do I have something to teach others is seldom the right question to ask. The right questions however, are two others: a. Is there someone willing to pay for what I know and can I probably learn how to teach it? b. How do I set up what I know into a course and make it available online? The good point about these two questions is that the answers to both are a lot easier than you think. One more thing! Given what is going on in the world at the point when I am authoring this book, the need and demand for Online courses and distance learning are and will continue just becoming more and more. To learn about how you can put your knowledge together and set up an online course in less than a week, visit the online courses section in the chapter 2 of *the companion course*.

Online Advising and Coaching

Online advising and coaching are just growing. People need help in both their personal as well as professional lives. If you have expertise in helping others solve their problems or deal with their challenges at home or at work, you can consider starting an online business. Building such a business is primarily based on your competence and hence needs a very limited amount of money to start. And again, when the world is facing one of its worst crises of the last century, there should be more need to help others. To learn about how you can set up an advisory or consulting business in a few days, visit the advising and coaching section in the chapter 2 of the companion course.

Online Shop

Starting an Online shop takes only a few hours. It is not a joke! It takes only a few hours. Full stop! Do you know what you want to sell? And do you know if you will have customers? Then it is really a matter of a few hours to open your very first online shop. Experts in this regard can help you find answers to all these three questions: What to sell? How to get customers? How to set up an online shop. You will learn how to set up an online shop later, in the "eCommerce" section in chapter 4 of the book and also the eCommerce section in the companion course.

Grow in Your Career

There are circumstances in which some may decide to stay employed, either full time or for most of their time. Learning entrepreneurial skills is something that you can use even remaining an employee of a business in an SME or Corporate world. There are at least three different types of benefits you can get from enhancing your entrepreneurial skills while staying at your current job.

The first is to enhance your skills and hence your value for the company you work for. In general, gaining skills can be for different purposes. You can learn something new because you enjoy it, like learning to play an instrument or learning a new software program because you like it. But you can also learn something because you want to increase your competence in what you do today. A new technology, a new software, a new language, a new methodology in managing your day to day tasks, a new system in managing your organization's processes and systems, and so on. They all can be beneficial to increase your impact and hence create value for your current or future employer. You can also find new areas that are useful for improving, expanding, and enhancing what your company does. If so, you are creating more value for your company resulting in the company be willing to return part of that value in some form back to you. Although there are always limitations in what the common policies allow a company to do for each individual. Still, the value you create, will not be left unrewarded, either in the current or your future company! Increasing your value and gaining new skills enabling you to generate more value for your employer is one of the best means to grow your way up in your career. If that growth pushes you so high, eventually out of your current company into another one or even higher towards starting your own business, because nobody is willing to pay you more than what you make now as a salary, what is the problem?

I am not an advocate of being naïve. Some people generate enormous value for their employers, their industry, and their societies. But are they rewarded accordingly? The return on your efforts is a combination of the compensation you get, the position you and impact you have, the brand and image you carry, and your overall satisfaction from who you are and what you do. It may not always be possible to get enough financial reward for what you do. Imagine a nurse saving the life of a patient. How much should the patient pay to the hospital which has saved his or her life? How much of that amount now is what the nurse deserves? It is difficult to give a monetary value to these kind of services. But if you are overall happy with what you do, what you get, and what you are known for, you may decide to follow your future by either owning a business or staying a valuable employee. In either case, learning more skills, especially the ones bringing results to your company is a proven way of increasing your share of what your company can achieve, and if not, you know what to do.

—

As I mentioned at the beginning of this chapter, this was not meant to be an exhaustive list of business ideas you can think of, but rather a quick guide for those who are interested in starting an online business but do not yet have any idea on what kind of business to actually start. For more information in this regard, refer to my website (link at the end of the book) for the communications where I will share content and ideas from myself and others on overtime.

Act Now:

Go back to the Course Downloads section of the companion course and download the "Business Ideation Worksheet" [if you have not done so yet] or save a copy of it on your device. Use this worksheet to capture growth areas you may think of for your business, or if there are business ideas, you can think of based on helping others grow

—

their businesses. What about your current job if you are employed? Are there areas you can improve in to be able to create more value for yourself and for your company which may result in you getting more out of what you do with your current employer, or a future one or be a way for you to go beyond and get closer to start for your own? The intention with this exercise is to draft the main areas you may consider to start an [online] business in. As mentioned in the beginning of this chapter, this is a short version of a separate potential publication as the process of ideating, evaluating and choosing a business to start is a significant one needed a lot of attention. Do use the methods in this chapter and this exercise as a starting step. Get advice from knowledgable consultants or other experts you may know to mature your business idea and ensure its feasibility from different angles before you embark on any journey.

Chapter 3 – The How

In the previous chapter, I have mentioned some strategies on how to come up with a business idea. In this chapter, I will show a roadmap to Build an Online Business. This roadmap can be used by all three groups. If you are an existing entrepreneur and want to bring your existing business online; or if you are about to start your first business and want to start it partially or fully online, or if you are an intrapreneur and want to gain this knowledge to help your existing employer bring part or all of the business online; you can use the strategies, and the method explained in this chapter. You may also want to learn these with the aim of becoming an advisor to others who want to pursue the road to build an online business.

Ideation of your Online Business

Before you build your online business, or bring your existing business online, you need to know what are you going to bring online? Both new as well as existing entrepreneurs find it sometimes difficult to bring their new or existing Business fully Online. In this chapter, you will learn how to decide on the scope of your online business. The assumption is that you start this chapter by knowing what kind of business you want to build. If not, go back to chapter two and go through those steps before continuing here. You may start with a list of few areas you may want to consider. You may change those during the process as you consider various aspects of building your online business. Even you may come towards the end and find something like a new idea or a major change to your previous one needing you to reiterate and go back to the beginning of this book and start the process all over again. But for now, ensure you have at least one serious idea – if not more – that you want to consider as the scope of your future Online Business before you go to the next step. If ready, then proceed to the next paragraph.

Let us see how you can build an online business from the business idea you already have or how you can bring your existing traditional business online.

You have an existing business or a good business idea. Try to answer these questions. What business are you in? Who are your customers? What do they need or want? What are you delivering to them as product or service which will answer to their needs? What are the ingredients of your product or the enabling components of your services? Who are your suppliers and partners? How do you reach out to your existing or future customers? Do you have a physical location like a shop or an office? Or perhaps you visit your customers at their place. What do your customers say about you, your business, your products, and your services? What do these customers need along with your product or service to be able to benefit from it? What do they need sometime after they have used your product or got your service? Is there something they may need over some time long after they have used your product or service? How do your customers pay you? How often, and from what channel? How do you pay your suppliers and partners? How often and using which channels? How do you stay connected with them also outside the regular sell and purchase interactions?

The answer to these questions is key in being able to go to the next step and create an Online Business. It is through the answer to these questions that the ideas on how to go online, will evolve. You should ensure that your answers are including the online elements you may need to consider and also have a good insight about your customers, if and where they appreciate more online interaction with you, your business, and your products and services.

Before exploring how these answers can help you shape your future online business, we need to also look at one more thing. And that is to see why some entrepreneurs and intrapreneurs are not successful in building their online business, despite all the efforts. These insights, together with the answers to the questions above, will shape the basis for drafting your Online Business Build roadmap.

You Are Not Online

If you are an entrepreneur with some online business, which is not contributing enough to your overall sales and profits or somehow is not as successful as you expect, or if you are a new or to-be entrepreneur doubting the value of an online business, I should tell you one thing. The point is that you are not online! You may say, I have the best website with the latest software technology you can imagine, I have a mobile App which is representing my business to my customers while on-the-go. And I am active on social media promoting my business on a daily basis. Or you may say that you hear similar feedback from some business owners and other entrepreneurs. But the fact is that having all the above is not enough for being online!

Being online is a journey. And any business journey has to start with your business strategy. Hence you should ask yourself the below questions first to understand if you are really online or not, and if not, how you should really Go Online?

Act Now:

Go back to your worksheet "Roadmap to Build an Online Business in 24 Hours." You have downloaded from Course download section of the companion course. Go to page 11 and use it to capture the answers to the below questions.

- *Ask yourself, what kind of business am I in? Is this a physical service delivery such as an airline or hotel, which by nature, cannot be done online?*

- *Ask yourself what parts of all nine components of my business model are already online? For those of you not familiar with this term, any business can be visualized by its "Business Model". There are different methods to visualize any business model. "Business Model Canvas" is one of those which shows a business's structure and components in nine elements: Partners, Activities, Resources, Value Proposition, Customer Relationships, Channels, Customer Segments, Cost Structure, and Revenue Streams. If you have questions on how to list and map out nine Business Model components of your business, you can watch the video on the Business Model section of chapter 3 in the companion course. You can also download a* template provided by Strategizer from the course downloads section.

- Ask yourself, in the components in which you have embedded online solutions, what is the contribution of that online element in the success of that component. For example, if you have an online presence in your "Revenue structure" – the last element in the Business Model Canvas – ask yourself what percentage of your total revenue is generated through that online solution or online product or service?

- Ask yourself, is your level of being online in all the components of your business model in line or above your peers like the similar shops, companies or enterprises in your industry, your country, or your region? For example, if you are running a restaurant, ask yourself what part of sales of your competitors are coming from their online channels like their website, their App, or via meal ordering services, such as Takeaway, UberEATS, and others they are part of. Finding the answer to these questions on your competitors can be difficult both for small as well as larger companies. But try your best. It is important that you have a good picture of your sector and the market you are part of.

- Ask yourself, is there any action or project in my strategic or tactical plans (or simply in my mind) that is going to help me improve the share and impact of my online presence in the areas I identified above? List all your ongoing and also planned initiatives and projects and answer this question by reviewing the list you have created.

- *Ask yourself, Can I reprioritize all my projects or intended action anywhere across the business by bringing up the ones which will improve my online presence in any of the nine components in my business model? Is there any new initiative that will bring more online presence than all the other projects already on the list?*

By now, you should have a good understanding of how much you are Online. Are you making money online? Are you having value-adding cost elements (ingredients, systems, or services you use) that are online? Are you having partners providing online services to you or interacting with you online, resulting in actual cost-saving or increased revenues? Do you have a value proposition that is purely or partially online? Are your customers paying you for the online services you have provided to them? Are interactions with your suppliers online? Are you having a high percentage of your support processes enabled by software and solutions that are helping your people and not adding to their workload and hence causing frustration? If the answer to any of these questions is less than a big yes, you have a need to change your priorities.

Revise Your Priorities

Now it is time to review your updated list of business initiatives and projects and think. If you are a solo entrepreneur, spend time to reflect and involve trusted mentors and experienced experts in reprioritizing your plans. If you are an SME or a Large Enterprise, trigger your strategy and tactical planning process. There is nothing more important than going online. Do not waste your resources before ensuring you have created customer value, business efficiency and resilience by building online enablers into all elements of your value proposition and business structure.

Although not all can benefit to the extreme from going online, this is the very first and most important business decision any company should take, both today and tomorrow. Yes, that is true for example, that airlines and hotels cannot replace their services with online offerings. But as mentioned, the need for deploying digital solutions and increasing your online presence is not only to create or add income (revenue streams). Such companies may well benefit from building an online presence in some of the other eight components of their business model. Think of remote working. Smaller office space has huge benefits to the fixed cost of any company. Going online with the processes that do not need the physical interaction of your people and your customers, can help a little bit now and much more so over many years ahead. Or perhaps education your customers to interact with your website and chatbot before they contact your call center can save you lot of money while improving quality of your customer support. If someone disagreed, tell them the example of the banks. Same people complained for couple decades on online banking. Today, apart from new banks born purely digitally, there are other traditional ones who have shut the doors of most of their branches and moved everything to their online business. The same will happen to many other businesses. Hence, do not waste time, review your strategy and plans, find every opportunity you can Go Online Now.

Create a Customer Persona

You have thought about your current or future customers in the previous steps of this journey. But to achieve a really great basis for a successful business, you need to go one level deeper. And that is to create your **customer persona**. A customer persona is a semi-fictional archetype that represents the key traits of your existing and envisioned customers. This is to ensure that you have a good understanding of your customers. Where are your customers geographically located? What range of age do they have? Are they male, female, or other? Do you know which religious or cultural background they are mostly from? What is their marital status? What kind of income range do they have? What kind of interests do they have? What kind of jobs or businesses do they have? What are their habits? And many more questions like this. It is based on these data you collect that you can decide what kind of products and services is suitable for your customers and what are the preferred ways of serving them. What kind of channels do they prefer? What part of your business can or should become online, and what parts of your customers may not appreciate going online? In the end, you do all this to increase number of your customers and their satisfaction.

Act Now:

Go back to your worksheet "Roadmap to Build an Online Business in 24 Hours." You have downloaded from Course download section of the companion course. Go to page 15 and use that form to capture your customer persona. Make additional copies of this page as many as needed if you have more than one category of customers where it becomes difficult to explain their traits and differences among them in one form.

Build a Customer Database

It may sound too early. But creating a customer database, if you do not have one, early in the process is crucial. You may not want to start selling anything from your online business to them yet, but you need their names for a different purpose. You want to ensure that you have a way to verify the customer persona(s) you have created above. How much each of the names on the list matches the explanations you have put on your customer personas? If you find names of potential customers that do not match any of the personas you have created, there are two possibilities. The most common one is that you have something to change and improve in the way you describe your product and services and the value proposition you have in mind for your online business. That is because not matching customers to the envisioned customer persona can be a sign that you are not having or offering what they want. That is a dangerous thing. But good for you that you have identified this risk so early in the process. The second possibility is that you may have created the right products and services, but your customer in mind does not fit that product or service. You either need to create an additional persona representing that customer or think if that is really a potential customer after all. Is that customer really going to open his or her wallet when you present to him or her your offering down the line?

This exercise is to ensure you transform the semi-fictional customer persona into someone with flesh and blood who will be willing to pay for what you have to offer. Moreover, creating a real list of customers from scratch or expanding your existing one to be used in your future online business is something you do not want to delay that much. A real business build exercise will always go hand in hand with real customers in mind as you shape every component of your business.

Act Now:

I have provided you a format for your customer database. Go back to your worksheet "Roadmap to Build an Online Business in 24 Hours." You have downloaded from Course download section of the companion course. Go to page 16. You can also use any other database or tool in collecting the information about your customers. But ensure you have all the columns of the format I have provided in such a database. Start to add the name of potential customers whom you think will buy your products and services, online. The objective of this exercise is to create a picture of real customers to ensure there are real people who are like what you have described in the customer persona's.

Sell to the World

Any great business should have Customers across the world! Not all businesses can. But think about it as a vision. Most of the companies which are present at a global level have created products and services they can sell principally in any country and any city in the world. They may not choose to do so. But that is their choice considering the costs and benefits of presence in each market. Think of Apple. If they did stick to a few countries, would they become the first USD 1.5 trillion company in the world? What about the impact of a crisis or a political situation affecting their business in a country or a region if that was their only source of sales? Would they not have been more vulnerable if they limited their markets to fewer countries?

Can you sell some of your products and services to the customers on the other side of the city, to the other cities in your country, to the neighboring countries, or further beyond? You do not need to make the entire world your customer. But make at least the world around you, so. The current crisis we are in as I author this book or other crisis you may face in the future will be behind us after all. How do you prepare yourself for the next one? The mistake you can make is that you take your next business decision without considering an alternative way which makes you more resilient by expanding wider geographically to the next village or the next continent.

Imagine if you are a good chef and the owner of a small restaurant. Being in the lockdown during the current crisis or facing other types of business challenges, you could still earn money despite your restaurant being closed. How? By delivering food online, or by preparing meal-kits (chosen ingredients or half-prepared meals) selling them to your regular customers for the period that they cannot visit your restaurant, or by having a website teaching your skills on how to run a successful restaurant for those who are not in the lockdown areas on another side of the world. You have the entire world – or at least the parts which are not in a lockdown – as your audience. On this last one, someone would say, what if everybody starts to provide such services, specifically training? Who will really then cook? Is this going to become an overcrowded space soon? The answer to this is a clear NO! First of all, this is one of the ways to create Additional Streams of Income for your business and is not supposed to become the only one. Second, this is not for everyone and every business. And third, the majority of the people asking these questions are also the ones who do not take such actions and stay skeptical while few others are enjoying its benefits. The point is not also that all of us should start teaching others and stop what we are doing as we do not want a world of teachers without anyone doing anything else. This is only one of three possibilities in the above example, to show why and how you should create a portfolio of services to create resilience for good and the worse days. And that brings us to the next thing you should do.

Act Now:

Go to your workbook "Roadmap to Build an Online Business in 24 Hours." downloaded from the Course Downloads section of the course companion, page 17 and answer these questions. How can you increase your target market? Where are the next customers you can target in addition to your currently existing or imagines customers? Think of the next village, city, province, or country. Think of another type of customers who may want a slightly different product than what you have to sell today. Think about how an online business may bring those customers to you, which you could not access without such an online presence. The idea of this exercise is to ensure you start to think about your target market with being online in mind. It is sometimes difficult to switch your mindset – especially if you have been running a traditional business for long – to think of your market in a wider sense than before.

Diversify

Do you have a portfolio of products or services? A portfolio of products or services can be as simple as a list of all different things you produce and sell or the services you deliver to your customers. But to diversify is something more than that. Expanding your products and services is not just to increase the variety of your products or services on your menu or your product list. Think of three things. First, what can you sell to your customers while they are purchasing one of the items from your existing portfolio? Second, what might the customers who purchased something from your portfolio need tomorrow, which is not on your list of products and services yet? And third, what might your customers need when they cannot buy your products and services? For this last one, use a situation like the corona crisis in 2020 as a frame condition to discover answers. Answer to these questions can help you find out how to expand your offerings and diversify your service portfolio creating more value for your customers and resilience for your business. Are there online presence capabilities that can help you create new offerings answering to one of the three needs above?

Act Now:

Go to your workbook "Roadmap to Build an Online Business in 24 Hours." downloaded from the Course Downloads section of the companion course, page 18 and Think of how you can diversify your products and services. Do not just expand your menu or product list. But think using the logic described above. What do your customers want while using the products or services they would be buying from you already? What products or services will they need after using what they buy from you? What would they need instead if they could not buy those products or services for a while (such as in crisis times or if their need or priority changes)?

Navigate the Value Chain

There is a saying that in the American gold rush, the tool sellers made most of the money, not the explorers. Being it a fact or a fable, there is a learning in this statement. Irrespective of success or failure, the gold explorers should have had tools and hence needed to buy them. Who do you think made more money, the explorers or the ones selling tools to hundreds of the explorers? Think of a company designing accounting software. Both people with great businesses and double-digit profit margins, as well as mediocre or even almost bankrupt ones, use and pay for the accounting software.

What does this let you reflect on? Designing an Online Business, you may not need to copy exactly what you have been doing in your traditional business offline; you may move in the value chain to a different point where you can get more income by less efforts – i.e.

less cost. It is also the same for you as a new entrepreneur or a to-be entrepreneur. You can reiterate and move in the future value chain you will be part of and find a better spot, even when you still have only a business idea. Building an online business is not only about shaping its digital components. It is also to decide the right place to be and the right value to deliver [to your customers] and the value to capture [your benefits and profits].

For example, if you are making some products, you may have part of the process which you have outsourced to others. Say, for example; you produce some ready to consume homemade dishes and sell on your web-shop. You have someone who prepares the ingredients, and also half-cooks them for you. You design the recipes, prepare the meals into boxes, and ship them to your clients. Increasing the size of your business by going online, you may start to think of asking the person preparing your meals to do more than just the ingredients. Instead, he or she can prepare also as you used to prepare using the recipes you create. You can teach them how to do that and also control the quality of the work. Owning the online business, the brand, and the customer base, you are less worried about your supplier starting for own competing with you. You invest in your brand and ensure you add real value via your service, preventing any newcomer, including your current supplier to be able to compete with you without difficulties. Now you have lifted yourself to a level higher in the value chain. You are now the owner of the business and do less in the operations. Just to let you know that some of the multi-billion world-famous brands do operate with the same model. Companies like Dell, Apple, and many more almost never produce the products themselves. They are more a strategy, design, and marketing company than a producer of what they sell!

Act Now:

Go to your workbook "Roadmap to Build an Online Business in 24 Hours." downloaded from the Course Downloads section of the companion course, page 18. Think about the value chain that you are or want to operate in. Is there any part of the work that you want or can think of letting others do for you? Use your business model canvas (access the template from course download section) as a guide. Is there anything on that sheet that can be done better or with less cost by someone else while you keep the existing frame of your business? Does bringing your business online or starting an online line of the business change the process so that you can outsource new parts of the work to others, letting you focus on new things in the same business? The idea with this exercise is to ensure you do expand your view on what your business is and your best role in it, to ensure you maximize the value you capture while sharing parts of that value capture with others (suppliers and partners).

Language, Location, And Logistics

A good business must be in English! And an online one, even more so. You can run a phenomenally successful business in your local language or another major language like Spanish. However, a non-English business limits your possibility of serving customers from around the world. If you have a good niche in your own or any other language, that is great; stick to it. If not, think twice before starting a non-English business as this automatically limits your potential audience.

A good business should also be doable from anywhere. Having a business with more locations brings more cost irrespective of your income or number of customers. If you need a location as part of the nature of your business – often called brick and mortar businesses like a shop, a restaurant, or a sports club – then do so, but optimize. You may not need all that you have today, given the changes in the world over the coming years and decades. If not, and if you are able to adjust your business structure and business model so that you can reduce the non-customer facing location as much as possible, do not wait a second. A location-independent business is what creates freedom and new opportunities to invest in what matters: your people, your products, and services, and yourself.

A good business should have no need for large logistics and storage. Logistics is a hassle. It costs money, and it also may bring the risk of loss or perish if you sell products that lose their quality over time. Entering a business that has zero or limited logistics and storage needs, saves money and time. Again, not all businesses may be able to live without logistics. And we cannot all start eating software or training content for our meals. But choosing your new venture and business decision, you should think about this first before committing to any investment in physical components.

An Online Business makes all three of these both possible and easier. It is why you should consider these elements before jumping on any business idea.

Act Now:

Go to your workbook "Roadmap to Build an Online Business in 24 Hours." downloaded from the Course Downloads section of the companion course, page 19. Think about the language of your business. What is your customer's preferred language? If that is not English, can you create a side business using English as your language, enabling you to capture more audience and hence more customers? Can a new language, especially English, help you grow your business? What would be the cost of running your business in more than one language? The aim of this exercise is to open your mind if who your target audience is. Given you being (or going) online, you can literally reach out to anyone in the world. Consider how wide in the world around you that you want to expand. Look into their preferred language and decide. It is sometimes much more than you can think of to translate and copy all the content of your online business in a new language.

Do Not Chase the Money

A good business should be enjoying Online Payment. Online payment saves the cost and time of attending invoices and payments. It removes the entire process and puts it into your website or e-commerce platform. In addition, online payment is also a way to prevent Accounts Receivables. Chasing customers to pay for what you already did for them is a painful exercise. What if they had already paid before they even got their service? Getting paid in advance in a high-end restaurant may not be even imaginable. While in a fast-food chain is quite normal. Selecting businesses that create no or limited account receivables is beneficial with the simple reason that you spend no or limited time to collect the money after delivering the service to your customers. You may also transform your existing business to be so.

A good business should also get paid again and again by having a **recurring revenue**. Think of your subscription for mobile or internet. You pay your monthly subscription fees irrespective of how much you actually use your phone unless you have a pay-as-you-go service which can become more expensive. A subscription fee guarantees a stream of income for your service provider enabling them to run a stable business and eventually invest with more confidence for the future.

You can benefit from the same logic if you consider online and pre-payment as part of your business model enabling you to also use recurring revenue models.

Act Now:

Go to your workbook "Roadmap to Build an Online Business in 24 Hours." downloaded from the Course Downloads section the companion course, page 20. Think about your current or future business. Can you change how the customers interact with you so that they pay for your product or service before they get it? Think of pre-booking on your website or App. Think of encouraging them to do with a small discount that is costing you less than the cost of invoicing, following up, and reconciling payments. Think of a subscription model where your customers can have a fixed monthly or annual fee instead of paying you each time you supply them the product or service. The idea of this exercise is to challenge your current assumptions on how a customer should get the product or service and pay. It might be that by changing the steps just a little bit, you create a pre-payment practice or online payment just before they get the service on the spot or a subscription model removing all the hassle of invoicing and collection.

Additional Remarks

The above list is not meant to be an exhaustive list of considerations on how you can make **the right decision** for your [online] business. But they were, in my view, the most important ones in today's world. These considerations are the ones which will extensively increase your chance of success and your resilience in dealing with the realities of what the future has to offer to you, being them challenges and crisis or great opportunities. To get prepared, you need to attend these. You need to create the capabilities or ask for assistance to bring your business and the nine components of its structure online. You need to define a journey on how to stay on top of the curve and benefit from the developments in this domain, which is helping many businesses grow and create more profits. Trying to sell to the world, you need to consider English as primary language of your business, think of optimizing your locations, and reduce or outsource your logistics. Keep looking for new customers in the next village or continent.

When diversifying, think of products and services related to your core. Having a basket of not related products and services confuses your customers and what you have to offer to them. Doing so is not even diversification of products and services but of your business and investment portfolio, which is a different thing. When diversifying your products and services, you need to have other related products and services which your customers want at the time of purchasing from you or later in their experience with your products or in case they are not able to use or get your products and services for a while. You need to use digital components in your service offering to be able to diversify as some of your enhanced service portfolio will be enabled partially or fully by digital components such as remote offerings, home deliveries, web content, and so on.

Trying not to chase the money, you need to create an online payment, recurring revenues (subscription or something similar), and advance payment as default. All these components can be easily or only achieved by Going Online. You need to create or modernize and enhance a great website to be present online; you need to be available on-the-go through your mobile App or a responsive website. You need to be on social media and engage with your customers. You need to create your online shop and start selling online. You should create online payment gateways to automate invoicing and payment, reduce or remove credit collection, and ask for pre-payment.

The one red thread through all these is in fact, to "Go Online". The more you go online, the more you create the possibility to automate and bring more online solutions to various aspects and components of your business. This creates enhanced value for your customers and greater results and resilience for you and your business. Hence stop what you are about to do next and do bring your existing business or business idea online before doing anything else.

Act Now:

Go to your workbook "Roadmap to Build an Online Business in 24 Hours." downloaded from the Course Downloads section of the companion course, page 21. As an exercise, go through all Digitalization of business models examples that has been mentioned in this section of the companion course. Try to think of their business model using the business model canvas. Then try to think what in each of these businesses is really online and what can be improved in its level of benefiting from being online. After this, think of your own business or your own organization. In which of the nine components of the business model is your company really online? In which ones do you have home for improvement? What are the possibilities to improve in those areas? Do you know all the available and affordable technological solutions to bring those components online? What are the relevant considerations from the whole list in this chapter that you should reflect and find an answer to before moving forward with designing your online business? Capture the results in page 21 of your workbook.

Chapter 4 – The Mission

Online Business Basics

If you are new to the world of entrepreneurship and thinking of building your first business, you need to build some level of online presence depending on your vision and business goals. On the other hand, if you have an existing business running a traditional operation, you can amend and strengthen it by adding a digital arm – i.e. an online arm - to it. Sometimes bringing your business online can be as simple as designing an informative website or a mobile App with the aim of getting new customers and additional income to your very existing business. Or you probably can change your business model in your current business by starting to help others in your industry – perhaps including your current competitors - with their business and charge them for high fees justifying the tricks you are going to teach them. You may also do this only for your competitors in another country if you are quite afraid of your local competitors learning some of your know-how and business secrets. You can also use your existing business as a platform to create a franchise setup where you have more businesses – i.e. existing or future competitors of you – start becoming your franchise using your brand in exchange for a monthly fee or a larger one-time fee. You can probably also start using your current business as a start point to create a second business linked to that. For example, imagine you run a famous local shop selling grocery. You may consider asking someone who already buys ingredients from you and prepares homemade food to sell his or her food under your brand. This way, you sell him or her some of the ingredients, and then sell the prepared food in your shop or online, benefiting from the profit margins of both ingredients as well as the homemade dishes. These are just a few examples of how you can transform your own business model by enhancing, amending, or extending it. There are many more ways to bring your existing business to a different level of income or profitability expanding what you do or modernizing how you do it.

One of the main prerequisites in being able to use any of the above strategies is to build a platform for an online business. An Online business enables you to achieve the objectives of any of the above strategies, both easier and also on a larger scale. Hence it is crucial to establish an online business structure before and in alignment with the overall growth strategy you are planning to follow in your existing or future business. In this chapter, we will go through the main components of the Online infrastructure necessary for any type of business. You can use each of the sections of this chapter as a quick start guide in shaping the related components of your online business, or as a trigger to improve, amend and enhance it, if you already have one. Each section also comes with a respective section in the companion course which you can use to learn about that subject before moving forward to the next topic. You can also come back to each section in the companion course at a later stage as and when you need to refresh your mind and rehearse.

Web Presence via a great website

The very first component of any online business is a website. Websites are the digital addresses of today's businesses. It is unbelievable how many businesses do not have a website or a proper web address. Websites are the very first things which give both access as well as visibility to your business. With the younger generation becoming adults, their expectation of accessing your business via a search engine like Google is like the expectation of older generations on having your name on the yellow pages of your city or by the call center of your national telecom provider. You simply cannot remain offline anymore.

On one hand, there are people who may argue that their business has its own permanent customers and hence they do not see any need to spend money on building a website. This is just like wanting to remove your name from a city directory of the past for the very same reason. The simple reason for being an existing business is enough to be needing to register yourself online. And that is to have a website as a minimum. Moreover, the cost of building a basic one or a few pager website and a domain name that is referring to your business can be as low as a few dollars a month. Hence, there are no reasons to remain defensive and stay hidden from the global presence directory i.e. the Internet.

There are others on the other hand that thinks being online via a website is old school, as these days, people use Instagram or other social media to get to know businesses. That is also a wrong assumption. Websites are the core of any online business for a variety of reasons that you will learn over the coming sections of this chapter. To name some, you need a web address to register for a business account on many of the social media platforms. To index your content by Google making you visible to the world through search [which basically is free], you need to have a website. There are official registries or simply local websites of your village or city or association of your branch that would list the businesses they know. And there, having a website is a meaningful thing next to your phone number. In the online world, it is only through your website that you come to exist. Moreover, people are more willing to touch a link on their screen than to call a business, and the easiest thing you can give them to touch on their screen is a link to your nicely designed "responsive website".

How You Should Build a Website

To create a website, you need a few things. First, you need to have a domain name. A domain name is the address which you will give to the world – and your customers – to reach out to you. This could be something like www.yourbusiness.com or something like that. To get a domain name registered under your name, you need to approach one of the domain name providers. You can search the Internet to find one. There are benefits in using the local providers in your own country. For example, they may accept local payment using your local bank account easier than international ones. You may also get more support from them locally when you need them. There are, on the other hand, other benefits in using one of the major domain registers which are active globally. For certain addresses like the ones ending with .com or .org and so on, you can use any of the domain name providers. For some others like the national ones such as .co.uk or .nl or .in and so on, there is only a possibility with some of the providers mostly the ones who have registered presence in your target country. Finding a good domain name provider is not that difficult. Search on the Internet or ask someone around you who knows. Visit the domain name and hosting section in chapter 4 of the companion course for more information about choosing your domain name provider and a domain name.

After choosing your domain name provider, you need to choose your domain name. You can get some help from the provider's website. They usually have some information to guide you on how to choose a good domain name. But some key points to consider are the below:

- Think like your potential customer. What kinds of domain names related to your business may your customers search? Which ones are easiest to remember or type? Which ones represent your business, your products or services, and your brand?

- Spend some time and search the internet well. You may want to refrain from registering a domain name like www.mybusiness.com where there is another one like www.mybusinesses.com already existing. This is more so if you have similar business with a comparable name who has a domain name very similar to what you want to register. Think of changing your business name [if you have not yet set up your business] or adjust the domain name you want to register for your business. There are some interesting examples. Think of the Korean companies Lucky and Goldstar. When they merged and decided to move to the new brand identity of LG [abbreviation of Lucky Goldstar], they had a small issue. The domain name www.lg.com was already taken by someone else. And their attempt to buy the domain did not succeed until later in 2009. You can imagine how much money should have been spent on purchasing this domain name. You may not need to worry that much. But with world wide web being a few decades old, there is a chance that you do not find the domain name you want available at the regular prices, which are a couple of dollars per month. Hence be careful in both choosing your brand and the selection of your domain name.

- Ensure your domain name is brandable. Your brand is the first thing many of your future customers will be getting to know about you. Hence, be a bit obsessive about what you decide to represent you. Your domain should make you stand out from the competition and present well who you are and what you stand for. This is how you help your customers remember you and your business easier.

- Think about how it sounds when you pronounce it in English, but also in your own language, or other languages relevant for your business or with an accent that the majority of your customers and your team have. Is it easy for people to recognize and understand it hearing it from behind a phone? Does it not sound weird in your local language? Does it not remind people of a funny thing that associates your name to it instead of what you want people to associate you with? Does it not remind people of something completely different, distracting their attention from you and your business?

- Think of a short and punchy word. What do you think of Google and www.google.com when you see them? What if they have decided back then to name their domain name www.theglobalsearchmachine.com. Would it have been as catchy and impactful? It is also easier for people to remember names like Google, Spotify, or similar compared to longer ones, which are more a description of what you do.

- The last part of domain names such as .com or .org or .co.uk, .nl or similar are called extension. Try to choose a relevant one. This is how your top-level domain will be known and how you can benefit from the right one. You can also damage your brand and your business by choosing the wrong one. The most common extension in the world is .com. If .com of what you want to register is already taken by someone else, consider other extensions such as .net or .info. Other less common extensions are not what I recommend. You do not want to put your business in an experiment to see if people find you by .food or .shop. Nobody thinks of searching for yourbusiness.food when they can think of yourbusiness.com.

- Get more than one domain! If you want to register www.firstname-lastname.com or anything like that, register also www.firstnamelastname.com or other variations that may be assumed to be your domain name when someone hears it. You also need to register the common misspell of your brand if it is a common mistake people would do e.g. when the brand is something from a not so common word or from a different language or a difficult to spell word. Register the most common variations of it. Also, register the same domain with the extension of your own country and also the countries in which you have customers or business presence. You will still use only the main domain, but you will redirect all the rest to this main one, which will lead people to the right site even if they type the wrong one or the other ones with local country extensions. Setting up such an automatic redirect in the portal of your domain name registrar is quite simple, and the cost for registering a couple of extra domain names is next to nothing unless you are LG!

- Do look into your local chamber of commerce and if they have any local guidelines or expectations to your domain name. You do not want to build your brand around a name and learn that you cannot use it for some reason after spending money on building all your brand identity components around it.

When you have decided on your domain provider and have chosen your domain name, register it following the simple instruction from your domain provider. One of the major domain providers is Godaddy. You can also consider other alternatives like Strato or others who are known for good service. But before starting to register your domain, read the rest of this section as it will help you in deciding with more knowledge.

The next thing you need to decide on building a website is the platform you want to use to create the actual site and its pages. There are four ways to do this. The easiest is to use one of the drag-and-drop website solution providers where you can build your website in a matter of minutes and have it live within the same day, or sometimes the same hour. The second alternative is to go to a bit more enhanced solution like WordPress. WordPress is a platform with which you can build both very simple, but also quite advanced websites. The third option is to buy ready-made website codes and install them on a server and modify it to become what you want. And the last option is to build the website from scratch doing most or all of the programming yourself or by your provider. We will cover all these four options in the following sections of this chapter.

The last thing you need for a website next to a domain name and a platform to build your site and its pages on it is hosting it. Think of hosting as a hard disk that sits on the Internet. These hard disks, or better-called servers, are called **host**. To enable people to access your website, you need to put your website content on such a host and connect your domain name to that host. Now your domain name provider will send all people typing your domain name in their internet browsers such as Internet Explorer, Chrome, Safari, Firefox, or Edge to that host in which they will see your content.

Why did I tell you to wait before registering your domain a few lines before? Because there are service providers that provide all the three services as one package. Being new to the world of online and websites, you don't need to deal with any manual setup between your domain provider, your host, and the platform in which you create and keep your content. In the following sections of this chapter, you will learn how to do all these steps in one go and with one service provider.

Simple website solutions

Starting your online presence and creating your very first website can be something you do over a day. Imagine you have decided what kind of content you want to put on your website and have a few pages of information as well as few photos from your products, services, or facilities. Do not worry if you do not have many or any of those yet. You can even create your website with some dummy content – i.e. placeholder for your actual content – and replace them with the actual content at a later stage. You can even keep creating your content over time and once in a while update parts of your content on your website. Doing this in a step-by-step approach does not result in any problem as the way the websites are built are meant exactly for this purpose and to achieve that, you use something called a **Content Management System or a Site Builder.**

Content Management System (CMS) & Site Builders

Do not get scared. Content Management System or as abbreviation CMS are simple software tools which remove the need for knowing any or most of the software and web programming knowledge from the user. Think of CMS as a Web version of Microsoft Word or PowerPoint. You do not need to know any software programming language to create a document or a nice presentation with some animations, and so on. You simply open MS-Word or MS-PowerPoint and start typing or adding images or shapes, animations, or other components by just dragging them from the toolbar or menu and dropping them onto your new file. You can also open an old document or a template file, make a copy of it and use it to create something new, preventing the need to build everything from scratch. The same applies to websites. You use CMS Software to build websites as you do use MS-Word and MS-PowerPoint to create documents and presentations. There are tens of different CMS software out there. Which one you choose depends on you and the kind of complexity you want to build on your website.

In the past, CMS's were being installed just like other software on your computer. But today, most of CMS software are themselves online programs. You just open their website, create an account as you do for creating a new email on Hotmail or Gmail and start building your website by typing your content and adding your photos, videos, and so on. You push a button to add a new page, and you link that page to a button on the previous page telling the CMS to bring people who click on that specific button to the second page you created. You can achieve a lot with a CMS. You may never need to go to software programming. And if you need it, that may be well in the future. You may run your business for years on a simple or even quite a professional CMS getting all that you need.

The CMSs are mainly two types: there are many of them which are so simple to use with pure drag-and-drop where you do not need any software programming or anything complicated, other than clicking on the components elements like a textbox or an image chooser and so on and start typing your content in them or add some photos or videos if you wish. These platforms are easy to use and will bring you far in shaping your website, and as they need no program code from your side, they are sometimes called **No-code CMS's** or better said **Site Builder** Software as they do more to help you build a site than manage your content.

The second group is more professional CMS's. You still do not need any programming, and if you ever need, it is very limited coding, and that is why they are called **Low-Code CMS's**. These groups help you more with managing your content, which means giving you the possibility and ease of using and reusing your content in different forms and shapes without the need to duplicate the content. You can also structure your content into folder like or similar structures in some of these CMS's to manage your content, and that is why they are called Content Management Systems. What you can achieve with these CMSs are much more advanced. You can build complicated webpages with much more components, and you can link these pages to much different other content sources such as databases and other software you may have or need via the integration capabilities of these platforms. The idea with these Low-Code CMS's is that you should be able to run almost everything you need using their mostly drag-and-drop and settings menus without needing to write any program code. You should also be able to enhance your website by connecting it to other ready-made software. This means that you are still editing content and structure and connecting different software with some simple steps instead of writing any code.

Beyond these two types of CMS's, are websites fully developed using programming software codes. There are also two additional approaches to build such websites. The first is to program everything from scratch. Second is to find or buy ready-made pieces of code written by others and start modifying them to become what you need, instead of designing every single bit of the website from scratch. More and more companies use the second approach as coding from scratch became unnecessary and time-consuming. You can find thousands of ready-made codes which you can either download for free or buy using a very little amount of money. For the purpose of this book, we will focus on CMS's only as this book is meant for basic to intermediate level of skills on online platforms.

We will look into all these possibilities in the following sections of this chapter but spend more time explaining how to build a website using a CMS, which enables you to achieve what I have promised: build your online presence in 24 hours.

Wix

From tens of easy, but very good content management systems, I chose to introduce Wix in this book. Wix belongs to Wix.com Ltd., a software company providing cloud-based web development services. Wix makes it possible to build websites using online drag and drop tools. The beauty with Wix is that you can start with a very simple website structure and look and feel and advance it as you progress. The start version is free. But you need to pay monthly fees starting from four and a half Euros up to thirty-five Euros a month depending on what kind of website you want to have. To start, you can simply stick to the free version. To build a website with few pages describing your business, showing your products and services, and your contact details enabling your visitors to reach out to you, you need to spend less than an hour. I tried to build a small website just before writing these sentences. It took me around five minutes to have the site up and running ready to type or copy/paste your content in. Adding your content and photos and setting up everything will need more time. But be sure, there is no code and programming involved and not a project of a few weeks ahead of you. To try Wix, go to Wix.com, create an account, or log in with Facebook or Google and answer a few questions to have your website up and running really in few minutes.

Create a Website You're Proud Of

Discover the platform that gives you the freedom to create, design, manage and develop your web presence exactly the way you want.

Get Started

When building your Wix account, and when you arrive at this stage shown in the snapshot below, choose Wix ADI option on the left side for an easier process for building your website. Don't think that an easy process to build a Wix website means that you have an ugly one or one with very limited functionality. Take a look at some examples of websites built with Wix so that you can see what the power of Wix is on the companion course.

WiX

CHOOSE HOW YOU WANT TO CREATE YOUR WEBSITE

Let Wix ADI Create a Website for You

Answer a few simple questions and automatically get a website designed just for you in minutes.

Start Now

Or

Create Your Website with the Editor

Start with a template and make it your own, with easy drag and drop & 1000s of design features.

Choose a Template

After building the basic structure of your website, you can always change its look and feel by choosing a new template from among tens of Wix template. This means that your content stays independent from your website's look and feel which makes it possible to refresh or completely modernize your website with couple of clicks without needing to change anything in your content. You can add your social plug-ins, e-commerce, online marketing, contact forms, e-mail marketing, and community forums to your website using a variety of Wix-developed and third-party applications. The Wix website builder is built on a freemium business model, earning its revenues through premium upgrades. Hence go online, take a free account, and start playing to learn and go online in less than 10 minutes. See the additional information on the companion course.

WordPress

The first question you may ask after seeing the power of CMS's like Wix is, why would I look for something else, if I can do all I need using a CMS like Wix? There are two answers to this question. The first answer is: you do not actually need to. You may build, improve, enhance, and stay with a CMS or a site builder as simple as Wix forever and not need anything more advanced to run your website and the linked processes and applications to it. The second answer is: you may want to consider more sophisticated content management systems such as WordPress for various reasons. Let me try to compare simple CMS's like Wix and the more advanced ones like WordPress using an example. With any CMS like Wix, you are using something like LEGO blocks to build your structure. There is the ease of start and much more advanced components you can add later and enhance your structure and its functionalities. But there are also limits to what you can build using these kinds of CMS's.

The ultimate freedom to build a website with any structure you need is through coding it from scratch. If the use of simple CMS's is like a LEGO-like structure, the pure coding from scratch is something like using bricks and mortar by which you can shape your structure to literally any form you want. But as we do not want and have the time to spend on building by bricks and mortar – i.e. coding - , we use CMS's which do the hard work for us and create the code behind the scene without us bothering about how that in reality works. Choosing a more advanced CMS like WordPress is like moving to use pre-fabricated components for the main structure but being able to do any customization you can imagine, plus deciding on your type of windows, wood, cables, pipes, and more. You have a bit more work to do, but you achieve much more and can have much more control over how your website looks like and how does it function. In the end, you are not coding, but you are closer to what you would be able to achieve using direct coding. Not a LEGO structure, and not building by bricks and mortar, but prefabricated pieces with ultimate flexibility and robustness.

This in-between solution provided by WordPress has become so much powerful and popular that today, more than one out of three of all websites in the world are built using WordPress. WordPress was launched in 2003 as one of many then-present tools for building a blog. The nature of the solution allowed many to contribute to its enhancement. This pushed WordPress to quickly go beyond its original purpose, housing immense capabilities through lots of plugins so much that major brands like Sony, Walt Disney, MTV, BBC, and New Yorker all use it for their online presence. Today more than 15% of the world's Top 100 Websites are on WordPress. An amazing number of almost 500 new sites coming to exist based on the free version on WordPress.org on daily basis and more than 17 new blog posts added to them every second.

Browsing the Internet, you will find two versions of WordPress: wordpress.org and wordpress.com. WordPress at its core, is an open-source and free CMS. Anybody can download the core of WordPress from WordPress.org website as a package and just copy it to a WordPress host service - which is a host that allows and supports WordPress based websites - and start building websites. On the other hand, the company called Automattic, which is founded by one of the founders of WordPress has taken this free and open-source package and installed it on a service they provide on WordPress.com. When using wordpress.com, users do not have to download or install WordPress on any host, as wordpress.com already does this. I would say wordpress.com is more like a version of simpler CMS's like Wix, but with more functionalities, compared to WordPress.org which is much more advanced with lots of features.

It is up to you to decide to stick to WordPress.org or go for a bit simpler version of WordPress on Worpress.com. My preference is the first one as it gives a huge level of flexibility in exchange for a little bit of more complexity which I believe you can learn and get used to in a few days.

WordPress Plug-Ins

WordPress has a huge library of Plug-Ins. Think of Plugins as Apps for your website. When you get your new mobile phone, you already have some Apps and functionality on it. You can just put your SIM card in or set up your eSIM, then set up the phone with few simple steps and start calling, sending text messages, browse the Internet, use the calculator, Take Photos and Videos, and much more. By installing Apps from Apple's App Store or Android's Google Play or other stores, you can enhance your phone's capabilities to unimaginable possibilities that even the phone producer might not have thought of. The same is relevant for WordPress plugins. You can achieve amazing things and create a super professional website by using a couple of plugins from the long list of free or premium plugins available on WordPress. These plugins are small pieces of software code designed by different developers in the WordPress community to add specific functionalities that are not available in the Core WordPress package, exactly as you add functionalities to your mobile phone by installing different apps on it. Plugins can be used to create forms, creating web-shops, or adding a course library to the site. The number of functionalities and what you can achieve with WordPress Plugins are almost infinite. See the video series in the WordPress section of the companion course to learn more about WordPress plugins.

Free Domains vs. Your Custom Domain Name

Most of the CMS's, including Wix or WordPress.com, provide domain names themselves. The domain names provided by these services have mostly their brand in the domain. Think of something like www.mybusiness.wordpress.com. You may start building your first website and play with it using one of these domains from the CMS you use. But be careful. A serious business should have an identity and a brand. You do not want any other business's name to be visible in your domain name. Hence register your domain separately or move to one of the paid versions of the CMS platform you are using, getting rid of the elements not related to your own brand identity. My recommendation would be to register for a package by a provider giving you a hosting for WordPress.org as well as a domain name. This way, you get a good deal while keeping a complete freedom. Even if you decide to drop your package and use something else or some other provider for building your website, you can always keep your domain name as far as you pay the yearly fees and comply with the requirements communicated by the domain name provider.

Ready-made codes and Bespoke Websites

As I mentioned before, there are reasons why some businesses chose not to use a typical CMS like Wix or WordPress and go for a fully created website independent from any content management system. Why do they do that?

Plugins

As I mentioned, plugins are great and add a lot of functionality to WordPress. They are mostly developed by third-party developers outside WordPress core team. Although this increases the capacity of building thousands of software codes resulting in unlimited possibility, they can also be the source of a pitfall. Plugins can break! Why? When different people write different plugins while not checking them with others, you can end up creating conflicts in how they function. This can impact the performance of the website or its functionality. Moreover, regular updates to the core of WordPress, may result in plugins to not behave as they did before such updates. And the developer of the plugin does not have any obligations to keep them compatible with the developments in the core WordPress as well as major plugins used by most of the sites, although in most cases, they do.

Security

Hackers attack banks as they know they exist. The same way hackers attack WordPress sites as they know they exist. The security risk is another reason why some businesses may not choose to run their operations on it. And when one website is compromised, the hackers may start looking for similar websites as the security holes in the site can be in theory found on perhaps many more WordPress sites who are using the same plugins or pieces of codes.

Updates

WordPress releases updates as your mobile device manufacturer or OS builder does. You need to update your core WordPress site in a simple process, which is basically to push a button and wait for few seconds. Although most of the website functionality after such an update will be intact, you may want to test if everything works really well. Some businesses do not want to worry about such issues and hence go for a non-CMS, or a non-site builder website code or a completely bespoke website design.

Uniqueness

There are hundreds if not thousands of themes you can choose to shape your WordPress enabled website. But many of these themes look like each other. Having a website which does not look like any other, is one of the ways to cast a professional identity. This is why bespoke website design is preferred by some of the businesses.

SEO

Search Engine Optimization is a process to constantly improve websites to rank higher in search engines such as Google as your audience searches for topics related to your website. Some businesses prefer to have their websites build completely independent so that they own all SEO processes, although WordPress has different plugins helping you optimize your website quite considerably.

Performance

You have probably recognized that even sitting in the same location – like in your house or office – using the same device – let us say your laptop or mobile phone – you get to open some websites much faster than the others. You also have seen that some websites are present almost 100% of the time you try to reach out to them while others are slow or they do not open keeping you and your computer browser waiting on a white screen or with an error at the end. Speed and guaranteed response are two of the major enablers of a great User Experience (UX). Using non-CMS based websites, you can get much higher performance, especially if you are dealing with thousands of customers or visitors who may use your website at the same time.

Building a Bespoke Website Designs bottom-up vs. Using Custom Codes

The days of writing every single line of code from scratch are over. There are ready-made pieces of code you can find or buy, which enables you or your developer to progress faster and get things done in a fraction of time compared to the past. As a result, the line between building a bespoke website developing all from scratch and using large pieces of custom codes is quite blurred. It is up to you and your developer to choose if you go for a fully ready website you can buy and modify or build most of the site yourself through coding. And in most of the cases, the approach will be something in between.

Conclusion

It is safe to use WordPress.org, and perhaps this is one of the best choices available when you start your online presence. It may take a couple of years or maybe even up to a decade when you come to a conclusion to move to use a ready-made code for your website or have someone completely write your bespoke website code bottom up. Do not jump too quickly for a more expensive solution as it may not be or become necessary ever. It is important to make the right decision. You are not supposed to change what you choose very frequently. Hence, look into your business plan and consider the expected processes in your business, the volume of your interactions for the users of your site, number of your customers, the role of your site in the customer experience — a construction company vs. an online learning company — and other elements when deciding to use a simpler CMS like Wix, or a more advanced approach WordPress or a highly customized and professional approach through a bespoke website.

Responsive websites

One last note also about **Responsive websites**. When the world wide web (www) started to exist, we have mostly been watching and accessing content through our web browsers on our desktop computers and later on our laptop computers. With the birth of Smartphones, we started to access some of these content from our smartphones. Later, came the tablets such as iPad or Android-based tablets. All these different devices with their varied screen sizes as well as different aspect ratios — the ratio if you divide the width of the screen to its height — created pain for web developers. Now they needed to check the size of each screen when the request for the site was coming from that device to the servers and return back the same website with the right size fit for that device being a large home screen or a tiny mobile phone. To prevent this pain, came the responsive websites. Today, Responsive Web Design (RWD) goes well beyond adjusting to the screen size. RWD considers other elements as well. Imagine you go to the website of your local authority to report something being wrong with one of the city furniture or equipment on your street. You do not want to have a large webform open, expecting you to type a letter about what is wrong. You may want a radio button type selection on pre-defined issues that you may want to report – as they know in that authority what anyone like you may contact them for – along with a small text field for eventual notes and perhaps the location of that issue in the neighborhood. Or you may even be happier if there is a button to record a short voice memo and send it to them describing what the issues are. Opening the same site form your laptop, though, you expect to have a place to type some information with ease and not needing to touch so many buttons as not all laptops are yet having a touch screen, and hence communicating with websites opening on laptops is primarily expected to be via keyboard. This is an example of Responsive Web Development where you ensure your website behaves differently, fit for what the customer expects, or gets delighted to observe.

Most of new CMS's such as Wix or WordPress take care of screen adjustment automatically. You need to add some other functionality to make any website more advanced in its responsiveness. But when you start your business or create your first website, there is no need to worry in this regard, as most of what you would expect, will happen automatically.

For more ideas on how you can make your websites responsive visit the companion course.

Using a partner to develop your website

Outsourcing your business processes should not be a decision you take easily. All your decisions, including these, should arise from a deep dive into your business model. For example, if you have a business heavily dependent on your website's robustness, performance, and design, you may want to use a professional service provider – i.e. a web developing company in this case - from the start. You cannot afford losing customers and not realizing it was happening for months in the difficult times of starting a new business venture. If you are Netflix, you basically are live and functioning on your website, every millisecond of the minute. On the other hand, if you are running a small business as a solo-entrepreneur in professional services sector or as an owner of a small shop or a small business or you are an individual opening a web-shop as a side hustle, you may want to consider building your website yourself in the beginning and perhaps forever. If you have lived with no major online presence for years, the chances are you can live with your own built website using one of the CMS's for a couple of years, if not forever. Hence, I would recommend you consider all elements of your business and its business model before deciding which route to choose. The process of deciding which way to go and if to use a developer or go for building the website by yourself is even more important than the outcome of that decision itself. You may consider consulting with a business advisor to choose the best way for you and your business to save potential lost business opportunities from a non-professional website from one end and wasting valuable money which you may use to do all the other stuff you need to do in your business, on building unnecessarily expensive websites which you can easily do yourself with something like WordPress on the other hand. Search the web to find a good web developer. You can also share your thoughts or eventual questions on my website (link at the end of the book) about choosing a web designer.

Creating Traffic through Social Media

Presence on social media was originally attractive only for teenagers. Later it became something for adults and then for small shops and businesses followed by the corporate world. Today, you see even a construction company having their customer only among governments, local authorities, and corporations being active on social media. Why do they choose to do so when they know they do not have any product or service to sell to regular consumers?

Just like any other development in the history of humanity, the phenomena of Social Media were, in the beginning, something on the side, next to the real world. More and more people and companies created their profiles and accounts on social media accounts such as Facebook, Instagram, and LinkedIn. This trend resulted in more and more attention to it and started a self-fulfilling prophecy. It was important to see what others did on social media, and then it became also important to be there as others did. Moreover, and even more importantly, this mass presence of people and businesses on social media was a wonderful place to grab their attention. And who needed people's attention? Yes, marketing agencies and marketing departments of companies. It went to the point that a new generation of marketing consultants and marketing agencies came to existence naming themselves Social Media Consultants or Social Media Agencies. What do they do? Obvious; they provide Social Media Consultancy (SMC), or they provide Social Media services as an Agency (SMA) where you can either get advice (SMC) or outsource your marketing process on social media (SMA) to them.

If you want to outsource managing your social media, go ahead. But if you are going to manage it yourself, or do it so for a while, then find the below information which should guide you in understanding and benefitting from the time and money you spend on social media.

Social media basics

The role of social media in today's online world is comparable with the role of word-of-mouth in traditional market dynamics. As you may have heard, one of the best – if not the best – ways to increase brand awareness and to create new as well as returning customers is word-of-mouth. People listen to people more than they do to the media. The irony is that today, the opinion of people has itself become a media – i.e. social media. What people believe is not necessarily the total reality. But what people believe determines how they decide. And when you apply this logic to a large population of people, like hundreds of millions as they are on each of social media platforms, you get almost a social consensus. People still think, judge, and decide for themselves. But given the free flow of information purring onto their heads every minute or every hour, they have the tendency to align their thoughts, judgements, and decisions to their subconscious influenced by the content they consume on social media. You have two options as a business; to misuse this phenomenon or to use it properly.

To use it properly means that you create a flow of information in the social media bringing the attention of your audience – i.e. your existing and potential customers – to you, your vision and values, your proposition, your business, and your products and services in alignment with what you have to offer them in the real world. This way, you ensure you are the first one they think of, when it comes to the problems you solve or the opportunities you create for them, through your products and services. This way, you use your message to tell what you are able to help them with; being it answering to a basic need such as food or health, or a more sophisticated value proposition like designing growth strategies of their business or shaping a great infrastructure of roads and transport systems for them and their children for the years to come. That is why even a construction company working only with the public sector or other large businesses would still go online on social media.

There are some well-established platforms on social media, each meant for a different purpose. There are also new platforms coming to exist or becoming relatively popular from time to time. Here in this book, we stick to few major ones which are the most popular and relevant for the business context and at the same time the largest with presence in almost any country and city you can imagine.

Facebook

Facebook, Inc. is an American social media corporation based in California. Facebook was founded in 2004 by Mark Zuckerberg, along with his roommates and other students at Harvard College. Today, Facebook is the most known and powerful social media platform globally. Facebook is also one of the most valuable companies in the world with annual revenue of almost 71 billion dollars [2019].

Facebook is among the Five large tech giants, together with Amazon, Apple, Microsoft, and Google.

Facebook range of products are way beyond its original start, offering among others, A Messenger solution, Video streaming solutions, Photo, and Video sharing solutions, and more. Facebook also owns Instagram, WhatsApp, and more. The power of Facebook on influencing the crowd has made it extremely popular for the business world as de facto marketing solutions generating great returns for people investing in Facebook Ads. The same power created lots of discussion and debates, as the world has realized how that power can be used in both political as well as societal domains intervening with the democracies and the order in our world. As mentioned before, this book is not about the impact of such a platform on society or ethics. We are here considering the proper use of such a platform as a way to boost your business. Hence, I leave such discussions for another occasion and publication.

You cannot ignore Facebook, or else you are not serious about succeeding with your business. Being active on Facebook, is like being active in the best newspaper you have had in your country or your city in the past. Some differences, though, are that Facebook is everywhere and accessible to almost everybody across the world. The other difference is that Facebook is relatively cheap. Although you can spend millions on Facebook Ads, but you do not have to. You can be present on Facebook for free and use Facebook Ads just as much as you find it necessary. If you do not get a good return from your Ads on Facebook, you have to change your approach and your content. There you may want to use advice from some of social media consultants. And if on the other hand you actually do get good returns, then it can become a money-printing machine where you put an amount in – as your social media spending budget – and you get multiple times in return – as sales coming to you via leads generated by Facebook Ads. The third difference of Facebook from old newspaper Ads is also that people always check their Facebook on average 13.8 times a day and spend an average half an hour on Facebook daily. This is not even the best news for you as a business. The best news is that you can target people who are more likely to check their Facebook more frequently and spend more time – read money – after seeing something on Facebook. None of this you could do with a newspaper Ad.

Hence it is important to understand and have a strategy for Facebook and Facebook Ads irrespective of what business, which industry, and what size of operation your business is in. For more information about Facebook Ads and to learn what you should do before setting up a Facebook Ad, visit the Facebook section in the chapter 4 of of the companion course.

Instagram

Instagram was created by Kevin Systrom and Mike Krieger and launched in October 2010 as a photo and video-sharing social networking. Instagram was acquired by Facebook Inc. in 2012 for 1 billion dollars in cash and stocks. Today Instagram is part of Facebook ecosystem but still appears as an independent service on iOS and Android devices as well as a limited functionality web version accessible via www.instragram.com.

One question some did ask when Facebook paid a huge sum of money to acquire Instagram was: why would you need an App like Instagram when you have Facebook in which you can do much more things than you can do with Instagram? This question is also relevant today. The answer to this question is not one. There are many answers you can give. Some of the most important ones are, to prevent others like Google to acquire Instagram back then. To get access to another type of audience who may prefer a more limited service like Instagram to Facebook, to access to more data which is the oil in the refinery of advertisement industry, to manage risk, in case of Facebook as a service or brand, got into any kind of trouble which actually did few times since then, and because Facebook had the power to purchase Instagram and many other reasons.

But why would you, as a business, need to be on Instagram while being on Facebook as well. Perhaps for some of the same reasons as Facebook purchased Instagram. You need to be on both to mitigate risk if one of them did go into any sort of challenge or trouble in the future. You do want to keep your audience on both so that you do not lose all of them if one got banned in a country or if one got into any sort of challenge as a platform or brand. You also need to access different kinds of audience. Instagram was up until lately more for business to consumer (B2C), while Facebook became popular over the years for business to business (B2B) as well as for the public sector. You also need to capture more data. You have techniques to understand what the return on investment (ROI) from your spending is on either of these platforms and adjust and channel your marketing investments to that direction, which can be different in different geographies, different periods, and with a different demographic population. For more information about Instagram, Different types of Instagram accounts, and to learn how you can set up a successful Instagram Ad and benefit from the leads generated by Instagram for your business, visit the Instagram section in the chapter 4 of of the companion course.

YouTube

YouTube was founded as an online video-sharing platform by Steve Chen, Chad Hurley, and Jawed Karim in 2005, who were all early employees of PayPal. The success of YouTube looks like a fairytale. Acquired by Google a year later in 2006, today YouTube generates 15 billion dollars of revenue for Google. YouTube has managed to become a successor for Encyclopedias and today used by millions of people to search for anything and everything, from learning how to change the hidden batteries of device's remote control to basics of quantum mechanics. And if anyone goes to check if they find some information to start with on YouTube, what you as a business owner need to do? Yes. You need to be there when they search for what you do provide. Hence presence on YouTube by creating content or having paid advertisement is a powerful strategy. You want to be where the eyes are. YouTube is an enormously powerful marketing tool connecting you to billions of users who spend time on it. It is an easy and fast video shoot, and it is free! The basic strategy on YouTube is to produce content, get ranked high, build a list of your visitors for free, and then promote products, services, and events to them. You should dominate YouTube!

To learn the basics of YouTube marketing see the YouTube Marketing section in the chapter 4 of the companion course.

LinkedIn

LinkedIn company was founded in 2002 by Reid Hoffman as a business and employment-oriented online service. Over the last two decades, LinkedIn has become de facto directory of Professionals, the most preferred website to look for competent professionals as well as a place for businesses to share their business updates building employer value proposition and targeting acquisition of talent. If you are not on LinkedIn as an employee, a business or as an entrepreneur; then you are not online losing all the potential benefits from interactions with other likeminded professionals as well as businesses who may have an interest in business relation with you in the form of their employee, freelancer, executive, supplier, partner, shareholder or investor. Today, you do not Google for these kinds of matters. You LinkedIn them!

The acquisition of LinkedIn by Microsoft in 2016 has just speeded up LinkedIn's domination in its space and brought it closer to other services provided by Microsoft, adding value to both individuals as well as businesses. Today LinkedIn is becoming more a professionals' social media. Even the layout of its pages and the functionalities of it is becoming more and more a Facebook-like environment but for professionals and businesses.

You do not sell potato chips or the latest hairdryer on LinkedIn. Instead, you sell professional services. How? By profiling yourself and your company. Creating a robust LinkedIn profile for yourself and a value-adding and representing LinkedIn Page for your business is a great way to get you and your business known. Publishing content targeting professionals or firms who may be or become interested in your competence or your products and services is a powerful strategy many successful professionals – both entrepreneurs and intrapreneurs - and companies use these days.

To learn about how you can benefit from some of what LinkedIn has to offer you and your business, visit the LinkedIn section in the chapter 4 of the companion course.

Twitter

Twitter was established by Jack Dorsey, Noah Glass, Biz Stone, and Evan Williams in 2006. Twitter is what is called a microblogging website enabling users to share short messages known as "tweets". Twitter has also become a social networking service as users can use it to post content visible to the public or certain people or like or share – retweet – posts from others. With the explosion of the use of Facebook and Instagram across industries and the use of LinkedIn in more professional settings as explained above, Twitter may seem like a second choice as a component in the marketing strategy of a business. But Twitter has its advantages. First of all, Twitter has a different type of audience. If you are, for example, in advisory business on the environment or human rights, you may find more audience and potential customers for your products and services much more on twitter than on any other social media platform. Twitter has this flavor of public, politics, development, and international institutions. But it is wrong to assume that twitter is not relevant for other businesses. According to Marketing Land, Twitter reported 702 million dollars in ad revenue for the third quarter of 2019, an increase of just 8% year-over-year. Daily users on the platform continue to tick up. But you need to understand if it is what fits into your needs or not.

How to choose the social media platforms to use

There are many other platforms next to the famous ones mentioned above. Since years you hear about Snapchat, and lately more about TikTok. Each of these platforms has its own pro and cons, its own audience, and users as well as its own market. They pick a particular market and exploit it and its possibilities.

If you are new to the world of Social Media, I suggest you stick to the main ones such as Facebook, Instagram, LinkedIn, and YouTube that I mentioned before. But if you have a good reason to also invest in one of the more recent platforms such as TikTok, channel part of your social media marketing budget to those, but never do this at the expense of reduced presence on Facebook, Instagram, LinkedIn, and YouTube. Social Media is a quantity game, and there are simply hundreds or thousands of times more eyes on the larger ones than the niche platforms.

Selling Products and Services through a Web-Shop

As mentioned before, you can learn to build an online web-shop in a matter of few hours. In this section, we will be looking into two types of web-shops. First, a pure and straightforward web-shop being built in a matter of few minutes intended to just sell certain products or services. Second, a more advanced web-shop built as part of your website enhancing its functionalities to be able to run a full-fledged web-shop with all the needed complications you may want such as product categories, services, virtual products such a downloadable content or access to some content through subscriptions, or assistance, advise and coaching or similar type of services in beauty, health, law, business, or anything else you can imagine.

The choice of what platform to rely on depends on your expectations and the size of your business. But for this book, I stick to the best choices known globally among the experts and used by millions of web-shops and which are sometimes also related to the choices you make for building your website. First, let us look at two of the best platforms for building ready-made web-shops suitable mainly for selling products.

Shopify

Shopify was founded in 2006 in Canada. Today, it has become one of the fastest-growing companies in tech thanks to the huge growth in the online world and e-commerce. Shopify claims to power more than 600,000 retailers and growing every day.

BigCommerce

BigCommerce was founded three years later in 2009 in Australia but later moved its headquarters to Texas, US while keeping its large presence and workforce in Australia. BigCommerce has grown to power more than 100,000 online stores across the globe.

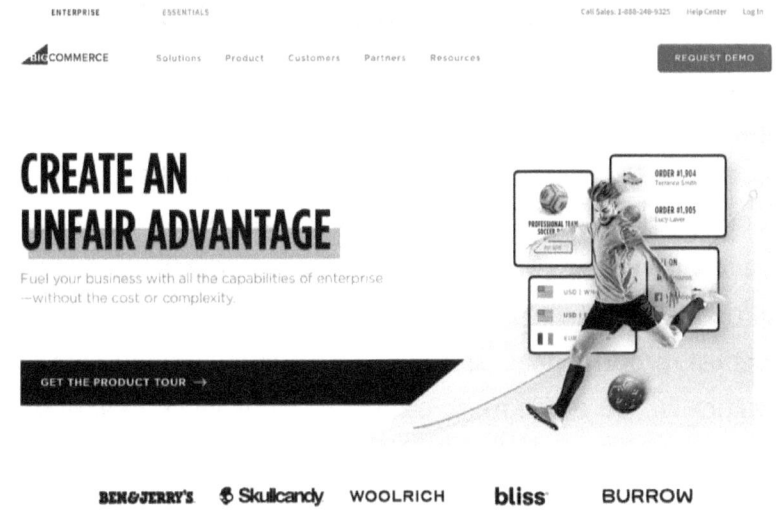

To learn how to set up a web-shop on any of these two platforms, visit the ecommerce section in the chapter 4 of the companion course.

WooCommerce

WooCommerce was launched as an open-source e-commerce plugin for WordPress in 2011. It is designed for small to large-sized online merchants who use WordPress as their web-site's backbone (CMS). WooCommerce has quickly become so popular due to its simplicity to install and customize and offering a free base product. You can build a great web-shop and link it to your main website or a separate website on WordPress only using the free components of WooCommerce. You can also enhance your web-shops functionality and potential by subscribing to tens of additional solutions provided by free or paid WooCommerce Extensions. WooCommerce is a wonderful way to start your online shop to sell any type of products and services including physical, virtual, subscriptions, or Bookable services. If you use WordPress to build your website, choosing WooCommerce to build your web-shop will become a no brainer! It takes a few minutes to install the free WooCommerce plugin on your WordPress site, which creates all the necessary site pages like product list, product page, shopping cart, payment pages and so on automatically. You can learn to put your first product on your online shop in about an hour and make money online.

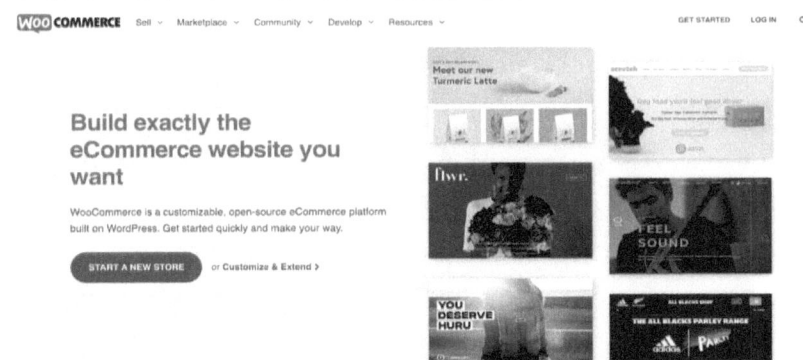

To learn more about WooCommerce, and a comparison between the three platforms above, helping you choose the right one, visit the ecommerce section in the chapter 4 of the companion course.

Setting up your Payment Gateways using a Merchant Account

Now that you have built your website and created your web shop, it is the time to make sure you get paid online when people purchase your products. For this, you need what is called a Payment Gateway, which is provided by Merchant Account providers or other institutions. Have you ever been buying something online or paid for a bill online? You perhaps remember that each time you complete all the steps, the last step is to fill in your credit card details or personal bank account information or your PayPal account username and password into the relevant fields on the payment page and confirm. What enables this payment process to function is not only the website or the web-shop of the company or organization you are buying the product or service from. There is also a Merchant Account Provider who is enabling the money transaction through the Payment Gateway you are using to put your bank account details.

Why? Why is there a necessity for a Merchant Account Provider? Why does anyone not build the functionality of payment gateways into the website or the web-shops directly? The main answer is the same as if you ask why people do not leave banks and work directly with each other. A bank is an intermediary enabling trust. With a bank in between, you create a ledger of transactions keeping the evidence of payments and their origin and destination. This simple function has been for centuries, the backbone of our economies. The same happens in the digital world. Payment gateways provided by banks, credit card companies, or other private providers such as PayPal are the intermediaries enabling trade by answering to the trust gap. This is even more important when the purchaser and the seller may not even know each other or sit thousands of miles apart. We do not enter to the newer concept of distributed ledgers such as blockchain which make the existence of an intermediary unnecessary. But for more than 99% of the world's transactions and for a very long foreseeable future, banks and online payment gateways are going to stay as an enabler for our economies as well as e-commerce.

To enable your website and web-shop to accept payments from your customers you need to add at least one payment gateway to your web-shop. You find some of the most payment gateways and how you can use them below.

PayPal

PayPal was originally founded and established by Max Levchin, Peter Thiel, and Luke Nosek in 1998 as Confinityis developing security software. They did not succeed in that and shifted their focus to a digital wallet. In the year 2000, Confinityis merged with x.com, the online banking business of Elon Musk. Elon Musk brought this company forward and focused on what we know as PayPal today, a company with annual revenue of almost 18 billion dollars [2019].

PayPal acts as a Digital Wallet. A digital wallet is a piece of software that can hold some value in it. You can transfer that value from other sources such as your bank account or credit card or it receives from others such as friends, customers, or other businesses. You can also pay for products and services from the same software. Digital wallets like PayPal bring trust as they sit in between your bank or other sources of credit and the merchants. They also bring compatibility and ease of use, as you can use them to buy and sell services without worrying if your card or bank account is recognized by the merchant or customer you are transacting with. PayPal makes money by charging transaction fees to the merchant and is most of the time free for the consumers unless the merchant wants to pass on those fees to the customer directly, in which case the customer would see this clearly before ordering and confirming the transaction.

PayPal was a revolution especially in its home country the United States as it was a great alternative supporting online money transfers and serving as an electronic alternative to traditional paper methods like checks and money orders. Today PayPal is an online payment system available worldwide. You can use PayPal personally, or as a business, standalone via their mobile app or website or better, you can integrate PayPal into your website with some simple steps enabling your web-shop to receive money online, while you are perhaps asleep. To learn more about PayPal and how to set it up for your website, visit the Payment Gateways section in the chapter 4 of the companion course.

Stripe

Stripe was established by Patrick and John Collison in 2010. Stripe allows businesses to receive online payment over the Internet. Stripe and PayPal are quite comparable. But they also have some differences. First, they are both online credit card processors. They have similar prices and charge 2.9% + 0.30 dollars per online transaction. Both support invoicing as well as recurring billing. PayPal is more known to consumers, but also businesses, while Stripe offers a much-advanced set of features through its developer tools. PayPal is known for its ease of use, while Stripe is known for its professional solutions in e-commerce.

You can also integrate stripe into your website or web-shop. To learn more about Stripe and how to integrate it into your website, visit the Payment Gateways section in the chapter 4 of the companion course.

Credit cards

Credit cards are the most famous digital payment methods worldwide. Although originally built for cashless payments at shops and other businesses by swiping your card into the point of sale (POS) machines, today you can use them to also pay for products and services online. This means that as a business, you need also to make it possible for your customers to have the possibility of paying with their credit cards on your web-shop.

To enable credit card payments on your web-shop, you need to use a payment gateway that supports credit cards. Both PayPal and Stripe also support credit cards. This means that using any of the two on your website, you can enable your customers to also pay with their credit or in some countries also debit cards if they do not have or not willing to use their PayPal account. Below is a screenshot of how they will get access to pay directly with their card. The actual look may differ from country to country or as PayPal keeps updating their platform.

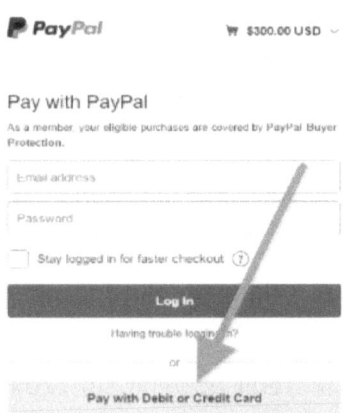

Local Banks

There are still people who may not have a credit card or a PayPal account. To enable them to pay with their debit cards (cash cards), you need to enable this on your website. One of the best options is to ask your bank where you have your business account. They usually have a description of how to enable this on your web-shop, which you or your developer can follow to build payment via debit cards on your website. This is even more important if you are in a business dealing directly with consumers or when you operate in markets where people do use debit cards much more than credit cards.

There is also the possibility of paying with local debit cards using PayPal and Stripe. But check for each country to ensure your customers from that country are able to pay as there might sometimes be local processes you need to follow to be able to enable payment with local debit cards via a direct gateway provided by your bank or PayPal or Stripe.

Apple Pay and Google Pay

Apple has introduced Apple Pay in 2014 in the United States, followed by a few other countries. Apple Pay is a payment method that can be used by Owners of Apple devices such as iPhones, iPads, Apple Watches, and Mac computers while they are purchasing both at the store or online. When purchasing online, Apple Pay works quite comparable to PayPal for the consumer. Activating Apple Pay and linking either their credit or debit card to it, customers can pay both online as well as in the stores using their devices without taking out their wallets or even carrying their debit or credit cards. Using the same technology (NFC) as used for the contactless pay by debit or credit cards, Apple Pay does not need any new setup or installations for the shops and other businesses that already have a point of sales (POS) device. Businesses can start accepting Apple Pay as soon as the consumers have them on their side with more and more banks in different countries enabling Apple Pay for their customers. There is a simple process of Know Your Customer (KYC), which every customer needs to go through by for example, confirming their address, mobile number, and so on to be able to activate Apple Pay on their first device. After this first authentication, they can activate Apple Pay on all other Apple devices they have.

 Pay
Cashless made effortless.

Google Pay or G-Pay on the other hand has been introduced by Google in 2015 as a rival to Apple Pay and as a solution for Android phones. Google Pay was also a successor to an already existing Google Wallet which was released in 2011. To be able to have your customers pay using Google Pay, you need also to activate that on your website. The process is comparable with Apple Pay. Visit the

Payment Gateways section in the chapter 4 of the companion course to find out how to set up Apple Pay or Google Pay for your web-shop.

Creating Conversion Funnels through Marketing Automations

Conversion Funnel is a term used in eCommerce which describes the consumer's journey from the moment of the first interaction with an online marketing platform or other e-commerce solutions onwards. Think of a marketing conversion funnel as an empty notebook in which you write the name of all people you think you will be able to sell your products and service to in its first blank page. As you learn about these potential customers, you take the name of some out and put the name of some others onto the second page. You may decide to look into the ones you know have shown more interest by asking you about the price of one of your products and put their name on page three of your notebook. Then you may decide to give a call or send these people a paper brochure of your products. The ones who respond showing some interest, are moved to the next page in your notebook for which you may decide to offer a discount if they buy that product within this week. For the others who did not show that much of interest, you may put them on a different page on your notebook and plan to give them a call just before the next holiday season when they may consider doing some shopping, including the items they have been once showing some level of interest for. And for the ones who already bought one of your products or services along the way, you have a separate list on another page of your notebook where you list them, for example, based on what else they may want to buy from you in their second purchase. And this cycle continues. This is a manual conversion funnel in its simplest form.

Imagine now you put all this into a spreadsheet like Microsoft Excel. You may be able to do more than when you have them on a paper notebook. You may be able to add more data about these prospects, move them from one sheet to another on the spreadsheet, create meaning for each of the sheets – leads, prospects, customers, returning customers, people interested in product X, and so on. Now imagine moving from an Excel sheet to a software that does all this for you instead of you needing to put all these structures. You just enter the potential customer name in and push some buttons to move them from one list to another, to add notes to their records, and so on. Now imagine the software has the possibility of connecting to your email software so that you can push the information of these potential customers from your system to it without needing to enter all the information manually. And then imagine you can also integrate this software with your website and social media accounts so that it detects automatically if someone visits a specific page on your website or looks up a product on your web-shop.

There are softwares and solutions that do exactly all of the above. Some of these softwares are called Customer Relationship Management (CRM), which are meant to help you manage your relationship with your potential as well as existing customers. Some others are called Marketing Automation software, which are platforms and technologies to create marketing channels and conversion funnels as described above. There are also a third category of software which enable you to integrate almost everything with everything else like linking your email software with your marketing tools as well as your CRM and so on.

At the end, it does not matter what category is the software belonging to as some of the new software, especially the ones designed for small and medium-size businesses do all of the above reducing your need to one single software to manage your marketing automation, customer relationship management as well as the integration of other software you use with these. In this book, I look into one such example. There are many other solutions out there. But I believe this software is a great start and can serve your well for a long period or even forever depending on the functionalities, you need and the size of the business you run.

ActiveCampaign

ActiveCampaign is a cloud software combining email marketing, marketing automation, sales automation, and CRM for small-to-mid-sized businesses. ActiveCampaign was founded by Jason VandeBoom in 2003 and today has an annual turnover of around 100 million dollars. Although smaller than some rivals, it is loved by more than 100,000 users for its all-in-one solution, simplicity, integration possibilities with other software as well as its competitive prices.

What you can do with ActiveCampaign ranges from the creation of awareness and intent in your potential customers, nurturing and educating them, converting those leads to deals and closing sales and support, and growing your customers and their account. The overall process should enable you to create an end-to-end experience for your users and customers. Using the Automations, you can customize what exactly each of your contacts wants, gain back time by automating recurring tasks, automate sales increasing your sales results, keeping in touch with your customers when it is most important, and present a professional business's behavior with relatively low monthly investment. To learn more about ActiveCampaign and how to integrate it into your website, visit the ActiveCampaign section in chapter 4 of the companion course.

CRMs and Other Solutions

There are multiple CRM solutions or Marketing Automation solutions in the market, each fitting for a certain type of business and a certain operation size. The aim of this book is not to compare those with each other, but rather to show you a way to build an online business in 24 hours. Referring to my website and registering for my communication, you can get updates about other systems and solutions which I will review over time. But the main intention is to get you going and help you make more money and reduce your cost by automating your business processes with a robust but relatively easy software to use. To get updates about different business topics and updates on other software and solutions, register on my website (link at the end of the page) to get the periodic updates on my publications.

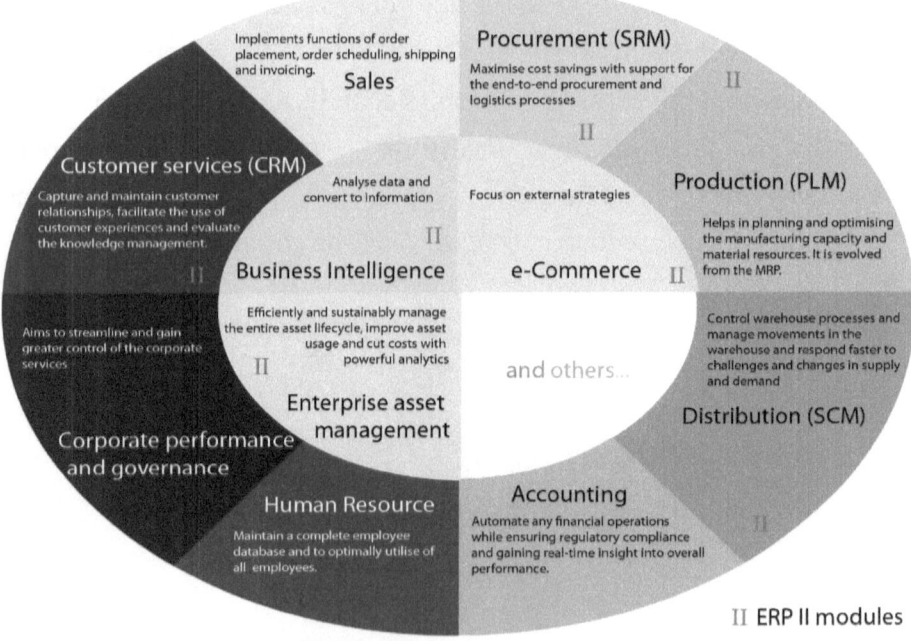

Reference: wikipedia

The Enterprise Grade Solutions

When you enter into the Enterprise world with large size and often multinational companies, you see other names for applications used for the same purpose as in smaller companies. All the solutions you have seen so far are also possible to be used at Enterprise level. But the volume of business, need for lightning speed response times, complexities of multinational operations, security demands, compliance, and many other factors encourage the Corporate world to use another set of applications to achieve the same objective.

But what are the main characteristics of an Enterprise-Grade Application? If you look for the definition done by different software vendors or experts, you find these specifications and expectations in common: a holistic approach on security across applications, IT infrastructure and business processes, Multi-level and lifetime control of data and files, High volume, efficient and fast data sharing and collaboration among employees, offices and customers of an Enterprise, Multi scenario ability to manage different user rights, offices, countries, departments and business divisions, suppliers and partners, customers and other stakeholders, Extensions and Integrations with other major business applications, management and administration of policies and compliance as well as data analytics and reporting and finally long term planning and enterprise-level IT support from multi-party support systems involving software vendors, solution providers as well as other suppliers.

There is an entirely different path to arrive at such a complex system effectively and efficiently fit for an Enterprise with hundreds or thousands of people, tens, or hundreds of offices in multiple countries and a complex network of stakeholders. Given the nature of this book and its intention, I do not spend time on the Enterprise-grade solutions here. I just added these few lines to give some hints and leads to those who want to start learning about these topics at the Enterprise level and pursue it at their own pace. To learn more about Enterprise Grade Applications, visit the section with the same name in chapter 4 of the companion course.

How to move to the next step

This chapter was meant to help you discover the possibilities for you and your business in going online in 24 hours. You must look at the content on the companion course. Each of the sections above introduces a topic and some software and solutions. It is through looking at the content in the companion course that you will have a good level of understanding of what these applications are and what they can do for you. After finishing this chapter and the respective sections of it in the companion course, it is now time to go to the next step.

Now you need to sketch out a plan and start the work! How should you start? What is the first thing you should do? What should you do first, and what can you park for a while? The next chapter is the answer to these and some of the other questions you may have at this moment.

Chapter 5 – The Vision

The way forward for those who do not have an existing business or are in the process of establishing one, compared to the entrepreneurs who already have existing businesses with no or limited online presence or the businesses who want to improve their online presence, making them more enhanced contributing to their sales results as well as their profits, is slightly different.

No Business

If you do not have any business at this moment, you need first to choose the scope of your business and then start with a completed business model as a start point, as explained in chapter 2. Go back to Go to your "Roadmap to Build an Online Business in 24 Hours." Workbook and your Canvas downloaded from the companion course and look into the business model you have envisioned and described there.

What are the elements in your business model that you think you should partially or fully automate, given what you have learned in the last chapter? Are there any of the assumed Partners with whom you can create an online interaction reducing the need for physical interactions costing time and money? Are there any of your key Activities that can be partially or fully automated? Do you need all the Resources you have thought of if some of the work is going to be done by a software instead? Do you instead not maybe want some resources to help you with choosing and implementing those software solutions? Or perhaps you want to start to do this yourself in the beginning? Is your first shot on your Value Proposition for your customers still valid? Or you have perhaps an extended, enhanced, or modified version of it as now that you are thinking of delivering the service in a slightly different way, using different (digital) tools? Are your Customer Relationships going to be powered by your website, a web-shop, social media, online payment solutions, marketing automation, a CRM software, and so on? What does that mean for what you have written on your business plan in this regard?

Did you discover new ways to attract potential customers to your business? Do you see new marketing channels? Do you need to enhance and adjust some of the existing channels as online solutions now empower them? Do you have the same Customer Segmentation as when you started this exercise? Or perhaps you thought of a new group of potential customers from a different segment that you can define a new way of working or new products and services for them increasing and enhancing your portfolio, hence your sales results? Is your Cost Structure going to be the same? Or you see now that you will spend fewer resources on some business processes and more on others? Do you see now a reduction in the needed manpower? Maybe some additions in the Online and Digital spending? What are your gains in the cost side that show themselves on your profit levels? And what kind of Revenue Streams do you have? Do you now think of new revenue sources because of all the changes above? Are Digital and Online going to be a revenue stream for you in itself, or be an enabler to increase your offerings, customer base, and hence power your existing revenue streams?

Reflection on these questions is the way to find the answer to questions such as How should you start? What is the first thing you should do? What should you do first, and what can you park for a while? You may find it necessary to get advice on finding the answers to these questions or in gaining confidence in the answers you have thought of yourself. Approach a competent business growth strategy and digital transformation advisor to ensure you are moving ahead with as much confidence as you can.

Old Business

If you have an existing business with no or limited online presence, you need to do a similar exercise. But instead of taking a future business model, you have your existing business. It is important to answer the same questions above, but with a difference, you should ask what the cost and benefits are of bringing an online solution in each of your business processes. Do you have a few large customers? Then perhaps a customer relationship management solution (CRM) is not what you start with. Do you have a business where people do pay right away after you complete your work in your office or shop? Then investing in an online payment gateway is maybe not necessary for now. Do you have a business where you should visit your customers and perform the work at their premises? Then a scheduling and rescheduling automation solution is perhaps a key priority compared to an online payment gateway. But one thing stays the same: having a great presence online through a high-quality website, and being active on relevant social media channels, having an online shop to sell or demonstrate your products and services, and creating marketing automation processes is always a must for every business. Other solutions helping you to release time, reduce cost, and increase your sales and profits, can and should be considered and added thereafter.

It is smart to do a proper business process review using your own expertise or of some other experts to ensure you have a good analysis of your business and of what are the highest benefits you can gain in each part of your business processes so that you invest in the right part of business process automation first. On the other hand, a holistic approach to automating your business and going online is also important. You do also not want to bring every piece of your business online with many separate solutions which can cause complications as well as an increased cost of implementation. Instead, you would plan for an overall vision for bringing your existing business online and hence a holistic approach to all its components. You can then define steps in which you want to follow that overall plan in smaller steps to manage the efforts and cost of implementation. Same as with people with no business, you can also here benefit from a competent advisor on growth strategies and digital transformation.

New Business

If you do have an existing business, but you want to expand into a new one and hence gain more customers, more sales, and more profits, it is important to consider the benefits of Online Business before taking any steps as was explained in the previous chapters. As mentioned in chapter 1, Online Business is an arm of your business which can enable you in different ways. On one hand, Online

Business can contribute to a considerable portion of your sales as its main or considerable channel. On the other hand, Online Business can enable you to grow your business without necessarily increasing your cost base proportionally. Hence, you should ensure you use all the possibilities of an online business model before thinking of any new business. This enables you to mature and drain all the benefits – read sales results and profits - you can get from your existing business first, before investing in any form for the next one. And when you do invest in the next one, you are sure your new business is an expansion of an already optimized and digitalized business that is sweating its assets to the maximum possible.

As an example, if you are selling products in your shop, first consider improvements in your business by improving different elements of your business model. Second, try to gain efficiency by bringing some of your processes online and by digitalizing them. Then think of how you can expand your customer base. Perhaps an online shop is a way to go before you think of a second branch. Then if you are looking for a second branch, a choice giving you more storage and less shelf space is a better one as you already have an online business that can really benefit from having a small storage and distribution location on the other side of the city. This is a different type of property you should look for compared to a larger shop giving you mostly shelf space.

Considering your business model, looking into improvements, going online as much as possible, then looking for any type of expansion, is a powerful approach to optimize return on your investments. I cannot overemphasize this.

Fitting the Pieces Together

Irrespective of starting from no business, bringing an existing business online, or starting a new online business, there is a need to fit the pieces together. You should look into your revenue streams, the products and services that are going to give you those revenues, and the share of online – or digital – products in creating those. Then you should look into the software solutions which are going to enable you to achieve that vision. When choosing your software and solitons, you should have a long-term view ensuring consistency and optimizing the investment cost. And in the end, you should go through your plan and implement one after another. You will learn and adjust as you bring your business and its processes online. You discover new opportunities and face unforeseen challenges. But you should be staying focused. And the focal point is your business plan. That is what you should stay loyal to until you change and improve the plan itself.

To fit the pieces of your business together, you should also ensure your people, your processes, and your online components are in sync with each other. This means that first, you should choose systems that automate work processes as much as possible. Second is to give your people a great experience when they are using these systems for the remaining part of the process which needs human interaction and hence not fully automized. You should also ensure your business processes are getting efficiency from the automations next to the ease of use of systems by your people. If you do not see benefits of automation, or your people suffer from difficulties of using a not so user-friendly system, then you are risking performance, efficiency and business sustainability which is taking you away from the excellence that an ultimate online business should aim towards. Use enough time and needed support in designing all three components in sync to ensure you are on a path of continual improvement for your people, processes, and solutions. That is how you gain more customers and keep them satisfied, increasing your new as well as recurring revenues and profits.

Advanced Technologies

The vision of creating, transforming, and improving Online Businesses is much more than just what you have learned so far. For me creating success for businesses using an online solution is more of a passion. Thanks to the development in technology, there is no limit to what you can achieve for your and other people's businesses. Let us look into some of those technologies before closing the last chapter of the book.

Robotic Process Automation (RPA)

Robotic process automation is a way for business automation using software. It is due to the nature and the role of RPA that this kind of automation is metaphorically associated to robots. In reality, there is no robot, and it is software that is acting like a robot. RPA usually learns how a user uses the computer to perform a specific task and repeats that using the same user interface as we humans use by simulating mouse movements and keyboard strokes. This is in contrast with regular workflow automation in which the process is built into the software logic removing the need for any human interaction where the computer works for itself for a while before completing the task.

RPA has few reasons to be used. First is that you may not yet have software which can do exactly what a human sitting behind a computer can do. Second, there are sometimes large investments in software in larger organizations that are not bringing the expected efficiency despite their positive role in the automation of processes. RPA used together with regular software is aimed at addressing this issue by increasing the speed and reducing the human interaction with multiple steps of clicks and typing and entering that is necessary when using a regular software on the screen. Either of these reasons can bring enhanced commercial outcomes, reduced costs, and operational risks, reduced manual work, improved user and customer experience, flexibility, and faster service.

It is not a necessity that you start looking into RPA as a solution for your business. But it is at the same time important to know it exists and to understand it. There might be areas in which RPA is the most efficient and cost-effective alternative for a major software implementation project or a massive administration processes or outsourcing. Moreover, you do not need to be an expert to use RPA in your business. When needed, you can buy RPA solutions as a service and have them installed on your systems, letting the solution provider help you improve your performance using the benefits of their offering while not needing to become an expert in the domain itself. To learn more about RPA, see the RPA section in the chapter 5 of the companion course.

Artificial Intelligence (AI)

In computer science, artificial intelligence (AI), sometimes called machine intelligence, is intelligence demonstrated by machines, unlike the natural intelligence we associate to humans and animals. The term "artificial intelligence" is often used to describe machines (or computers) that mimic "cognitive" functions that humans associate with the human mind, such as "learning" and "problem-solving" (reference: Wikipedia)

Using AI, we can simulate part of what we humans do, to be done by computers. Below are some examples of what you can achieve using AI. And if you did not already know, you have perhaps been already using AI for some time, without you noticing it.

AI-powered predictions

AI-powered predictions are everywhere these days. You search for something on the internet. You type a couple of words and suddenly, you see the full term that you have been looking for is there for you to click on, or press Return/Enter key and go! How did the computer understand what you have been looking for if you have never searched that term before? Apart from learning what all other people are searching for across the globe, today's software technologies are able to understand the relation between words using some mathematical algorithms. This enables the software to guess what the third word might be in your search phrase after you have typed two of them already because it has seen many did the same before or because using mathematical algorithms, it has found this word relevant to the first two. This is a form of AI. Recently, you have also seen the same in the latest updates to the operating systems on your mobile devices. If you run the latest versions of Apple's iOS, you have perhaps noticed that the phone already suggests a few things you can do when you go to the search page and before even typing any single letter. The software built into the iOS looks into the history of what you have been doing and also many other parameters like the weather, time of the day, and much more and predicts what you might be needing to do at this point in time. For example, if you have sent a message to your partner for the last few days around 16:00 telling him or her you are getting onto the road to come home, the phone is suggesting you now to send a message to him or her without you even thinking to do so. That is a form of AI which purely operates on mathematical models and not some sort of magic.

What can you do with this if you are not a software programmer? You just enjoy it! Learn about how it behaves and think if something similar can be of any help for your business. Then go to a business consultant and ask for solutions helping you with using AI to solve that problem you want to solve using AI. The consultants should analyze your problem and use AI experts to find out if there are ready-made solutions addressing those kinds of needs.

Learn from Spam Filters and Email categorizations

Today, almost all email providers have a solution to move all emails, which seem to be spam into another folder called Spam or Junk Folder. In addition, more and more email providers can also put your emails into different categories as they arrive in your mailbox. The two examples below from Microsoft and Google are the most famous ones. As you can see, Microsoft Outlook categorized the emails into Focused and Other. Gmail does the same into Primary, Social, and Promotions tabs. This is done to help you find the most important emails in one place and the rest, which you may not want to look at frequently other tabs. AI is what is enabling this by looking into some parameters like the sender of the email, its content, and structure, and over time learning what belongs to which tab.

Microsoft Outlook (Web version)

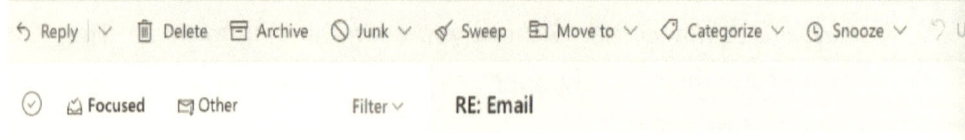

Gmail

What can you do with this knowledge as a business owner? Enjoy it! And then see if such a functionality is something you can benefit from if it is built somewhere in your business processes. Do you have a large number of emails or files coming to you on a daily basis? Do you want to sort them out by an AI-powered software before your people get into work and take action on them? You can bring this as a subject to your own software team or your business consultant, asking for a solution. There are ready-made solutions out there that can help you achieve things through AI that you may not imagine to be possible.

Translations, Transcriptions and More

Another way that AI can help you greatly is with understanding the text, the context of what is written in there, and also change that text into another language or another form of information. Google Translate or any other similar software use exactly this capability to understand words, the phrases, and the sentences and translate them to any other language.

There are also software solutions that can take your voice as you speak or a recorded voice and change it to text by transcribing what they hear. You can use this to capture content in multiple forms for different purposes or to use it as part of your business process by for example, being able to search into the conversations you have had and finding out business opportunities by looking into the key customer problems being mentioned regularly in different conversations. Irrespective of what you want to do with these recordings, it is always a good practice and also needed by law in most jurisdictions to get people's consent before recording anything.

You should keep such content only for the duration necessary or agreed with the parties.

The capabilities of AI in this domain is just increasing exponentially. Translation and Transcription are not anymore, the big surprises. Today, AI can caption your videos in multiple languages for free, get a video and change it to a text document as well as an audio file creating multiple forms of a piece of content, or the other way around, to get a text and read it out loud for you with an accent which gets better day by day. You can for example, write an article or a copy for your business or for your advertisement and have it read by AI and not your own voice if you wish to do so. Some of these functionalities are available for free and some with really reasonable price levels.

Chatbots

An Internet bot, web robot, robot or simply bot, is a software application that runs automated tasks over the Internet. Typically, bots perform tasks that are simple and repetitive, much faster than a person could. (Reference: Wikipedia)

A chatbot is a type of bot, which simulates human interaction with end-users on websites or Apps using a chat interface. A chatbot can perform a conversation with your customer or visitors of your website, just as a real person does. Chatbot can ask questions, answer customer queries and do more either based on pre-defined logic, or using Artificial Intelligence (AI).

What can you do as a business owner with a chatbot? Use one on your website! There are ready made services available which you can buy, and have it connected to your website. These chatbots take care of the first level of interaction with your customers and forward those needing more a human assistance to you or your team. To see how a chatbot can be used for your business, look at the chatbot section in the chapter 5 of the companion course.

Voice Assistants

Voice assistances are another great way of using AI technology. Today, you have them on almost any major IT platform: Alexa from Amazon, Siri from Apple, Cortana from Microsoft, Google Assistant from Google, MB from Daimler, and more. Voice Assistants help users to interact with devices without a need to type as for some devices like mobile phones the typing can be slow compared to a regular computer keyboard or not safe when using them on the go or on devices like Smart speakers where there are no keyboards at all.

What can you do as a business owner with voice assistants? Build one! You can use the available technology to build actions your customers can take when using your mobile App for example, without needing to type anything. You can also sell your products on platforms like Amazon and benefit from the already built-in functionalities of Alexa as consumers can reorder what they have bought before, simply by their voice on Amazon devices. Moreover, Amazon and other voice assistants have a library of tools that you can use to promote your business. If you have a customer based in the United States or other countries where there is a high number of owners of Amazon (or other Alexa powered) speakers, think of creating an "Amazon Alexa Skill". These Skills are like the Apps on your mobile devices. Activating them on your smart speaker is like installing an App on your mobile phone. By asking your customers to activate your developed Skill on their devices you may be able to interact with them by providing valuable content to them while opening another channel for interacting with them. Look into the library of Skills on Amazon to get some idea on how you may be able to benefit from building one for your own business.

See the Voice Assistant section in chapter 5 of the companion course to learn more about Amazon Alexa skills and its use for your business.

There is more!

The beauty of all the above technologies is that you do not need to bother about how they work. You need to know they exist, find out the ways you may be able to benefit from them in your business and ask for help from experts to utilize them in your own business creating more visibility, leads, sales from one side and to create efficiency and cost savings from the other side.

The Technologies and use cases mentioned in this chapter are only the tip of the iceberg. You will be blown away when you discover what is possible today using the already available technology and solutions at reasonable cost levels. I will be updating and enhancing this part of the book in its future editions, adding more and more use cases as well as new technologies as they become available for your businesses. Hence, stay tuned by registering your book by joining the companion course_and subscribe to my publications on my website (link at the end of the book) to get its future updates and other information that I will be sharing over time.

Service Automation and Future of work

Before closing this last chapter, let us also spend a few minutes on the Service Automation and its impact on the Future of Work. This topic in itself deserves a separate publication or even a research program. But I think we cannot leave this section before addressing this topic at all.

There are people in favor of automation and digitalization. There are also who are strongly against it. Automation and Digitalization are a great way to bring what we enjoy to more in the world, giving them access to food, health, education, and more. At the same time, automation and digitalization can result in losing employment opportunities as jobs of the past being replaced by the machines and software of the future. But if you think about it, today is neither of the two or a combination of two. We have industries in which there is a very limited amount of automation and digitalization, while in others, we are close to full automation, removing the need for our interaction with the machines to have things functioning. Examples range from Robotic stock trading software to fully automated metro systems of a whole city, removing the need for traders and train drivers and many other professions of the past.

Moreover, the point about sustainability plays a significant role in this dilemma. Some of the automation can reduce waste. Digitalization can result in for example, less use of papers or in a reduced need for physical business travels. But in some other cases, increased digitalization results in increased energy consumption due to for example, need for more and more data centers consuming vast amounts of energy.

The social and political systems of every country, region, and also global fora are the places in order to debate and find the best balance going forward. At the same time, businesses need to be conscious and sensitive to the impact of their decisions. Being it impacts on the local as well as the global employment market, the society and how it functions, or the environmental consequences of such decisions. Small and medium-size businesses are also part of such a socio-economic ecosystem. However, their challenge is on a different scale. As I finish writing this book, the world is struggling with the second wave of coronavirus and its impact on our societies and businesses. Automation and digitalization can help creating resilience for the existing businesses in these difficult times. Moreover, knowledge about what Online Businesses can achieve gives people and existing and future entrepreneurs insights into what they can achieve through different means and infrastructure than they may have been learning all their lives. It also prevents people from entering into traditional business models while they have alternative ones giving them more for less. I hope this book has helped you to have similar reflections taking the best decisions for your first or next business venture.

What Can You Do Next

As mentioned before, this book is a dynamic guideline for you to start your online business in 24 hours. But it is not going to end there. We have started by looking into why you should start an online business and more so during these times. We have touched on how you should find your golden opportunity to build an online business, how much online your business can become, and if it is going to cost a reasonable amount of investment. Then we have looked at the What for those who intend to build an online business but not yet decided what business to start. We have looked at different options you have such as selling your own products and services, the ones from others, or other areas in which you can build an online business.

We also have looked into the How where you have started with ideating your business, understanding why your current online business might not be successful, and what you need to do to change the situation. We also looked at the impact of understanding your customer persona better and start early to create a database of all your existing and potential customers. We also mentioned the importance of expanding to the world around you, diversification of your products, and your customers as well as finding the right point in the value chain for you to position yourself on.

Then we moved onto the Mission, where you have learned about all the significant components of a successful online business from web and social media presence to creation of web-shops and online payment gateways. We have also looked into the benefits and the necessities of marketing automation. Then we moved onto the vision looking into your vision for your business being it non-existent, old, or new. We also looked into how you should fit all the pieces together.

In the end, we looked into some of the more advanced technologies which are available to you at a very reasonable cost and with almost no technological competence necessary. We have also looked into the impact of service automation and the future of work.

From now on, this book will serve you a different purpose. Use this book and the online companion course coming with it as a reference. Go back to each chapter and section when you need to refresh your mind about that particular subject or when you have a decision in that domain to take. Ensure to watch the relevant section in the companion course as also the content there gets updated from time to time. If you need any information about any of the subjects, I will be more than happy to respond if you post your questions on my website. I will provide you with the best reference I can think of, trying to help you in your decision for your next online business build journey!

Success!

Appendixes

Build An Online Business in 24 Hours Free Companion Course

This is a **dynamic book**. By purchasing this book, you have also gotten access to all its future updates which I may create once in a while. I will add content, review, and update the existing ones and provide more strategies and techniques over time. All this will be at your reach, at no additional cost!

This book comes with a FREE companion course. During reading the book, you will see references to the content sitting in the companion course. To access the course contents, the companion workbook, the business ideation worksheet and to be able to benefit from all future updates and enhancements of this book, remember to register your book by signing up for the companion course.

URL:

https://shahrammaralani.teachable.com/p/build-an-online-business-in-24-hours/

You can also access the course from my website:

www.shahrammaralani.com

You can complete the book also without the companion course. But you will find additional information and some multimedia content which is intended to enhance your learning experience.

Contact and Subscription

To send any comments, reviews, questions or suggestions about the book, please go to my website:

www.shahrammaralani.com/contact

If you want to get updates on my articles and publications please register yourself at

www.shahrammaralani.com/subscribe

About The Author

Shahram G. Maralani is a senior manager with more than two decades of experience in the corporate world with a multi-discipline competence in business and technology. Being passionate about Digital Transformation and its impact on Entrepreneurship, Business and Strategy, he studies developments in the Technology and its role in transforming businesses and societies.

Before the last seventeen years with DNV GL in the TIC industry, he has been working for different industries such as Automotive, Management Consulting and Investment Banking. He has dual studies in Mechanical Engineering and Business Management. After seven years of middle and high school in the Iranian National Organization for Development of Exceptional Talents (NODET), he continued his education studying Mechanical Engineering in Tehran University and later an MBA program from the same school. He has been through different Executive Leadership as well as a Digital Transformation programs with INSEAD and Berkley, arranged by DNV GL.

Since 2013, he lives and works in The Netherlands after a few years in Dubai where he had his previous assignments in the Middle East. To learn more about him, you may visit his LinkedIn profile.

Back cover

Building an online business is a journey. But it does not need to be long and painful. Building a robust and future proof IT infrastructure should be part of a wider business strategy. At the same time, building an Online Business or Transforming an existing one Digitally, should not become a sophisticated paper exercise. Creating value for the customers and other stakeholders should remain as the aim of any business process including the Digital Transformation. This is more so for smaller businesses.

This book aims to inspire and show a roadmap to bring your existing or future business online in a short period of time. This process for very small businesses can be as short as few days. That is why the name of the book. Using the available technology and off-the-shelf solutions can enable you bring your business online literally in 24 hours.

Larger companies may need more time in achieving what they need. But the approach is the same. Study well what is available in the market, before digging a deep hole by never-ending studies, instead of taking real action.

This is even more important during the current crisis in 2020 when the 1st edition of this book is being published. More and more businesses are in need for quick but robust ways to ensure their survival. I hope this book can give you some help in doing so.

Shahram G. Maralani